Island Planet

A Survival Guide for The End of the Fossil Fuel World

Matthew Henley

PublishAmerica
Baltimore

ISBN: 1-4137-7119-X
PUBLISHED BY PUBLISHAMERICA, LLLP
www.publishamerica.com
Baltimore

Printed in the United States of America

This book is dedicated to President Oscar Temaru, the first Polynesian President of Polynesia, a rare individual of humility stature and wisdom.

Contents

Foreword   9

Part One
Conditions

1. **Yesterday and Today**   **13**
   Headlines   13
2. **Too Many**   **19**
   Religion's Role and Responsibility   21
   Change government policies that encourage large families   22
3. **Today and Tomorrow**   **23**
   In a nutshell   24
   Large Scale Environmental Effects of Fossil Fuel Usage   28
4. **The Energy Wars**   **32**
   The Energy Fast   43

Part Two
Solutions

5. **The Arcadian Protocol**   **49**
   Arcadian Project   53
   Enlightenment of the Mind of Mankind   54
   Arcadia in Context   56
   Virtual Arcadia and Its Implications   56
   Seeds of a Better Future   58
6. **Terraforming and Social Engineering**   **61**
   Reduce the population   62
   Responsible Altruistic Self Interest   62
   Economically Self-Justifying   62
   Responsible Consideration   63
   In order to win the war and build Arcadia, we must
       think outside the box   63
   Corporate Co-operation   64
   Nationalization of Critical and Important Services
       versus Conversion to Not for Profit Status   65

Plant Trees   68
One Planet   69
The need for a global nationalistic identity and ethic   71
The responsibilities for nation-states, longer-term stewardship
    thinking and appropriate legislation   72
Role of education   75
General Philosophy   77

7. Energy and Resource Management   **79**
State of the Fossil Fuel Resource   79
Conservation   **83**
Hybrids   84
Arcadian Hybrid   85
Hybrid Specifications Based on Technology Available Now   86
90 M.P.G. Diesels   90
Home and Business Conservation   92
Energy Alternatives   **93**
Hydrogen and Fuel Cells   93
All Electric Vehicles   94
Liquefied Gas   95
Integrated Bio Stream Energry Conversion Facility IBSEC 1   95
Liquid Waste   96
Localized Energy Support Bio Mass Cropping   96
Bio Mass Gasification Unit   96
Combined Approximate Yeilds Per Day   97
Bio Fuels   98
Ethanol   98
Bio-Diesel   99
Integration of Bio-Fuels Production Facilities   101
Thermal Chemical Conversion   101
Water Fuel Technologies   103
Water and the Bio-Fuel Initiatives   104
Pyrolysis Fuels   106
Alternate Chemistry Fuels   107
Water   108
Fuel Solutions   109
Major Alternatives for Electrical Generation   **109**
Solar   109
Wind   111

Nuclear 111
Hydro 112
Geo-thermal 112
Electrical Energy Policy 113

8. **Other Arcadian Technologies** **115**
   Genetic Engineering 115
   Fresh Water 116
   MarineTechnology 117
   Trains 118

Part Three
Anticipation

9. **Self Sufficiency Regimes and Preparations in Anticaption,**
   the return to an Agrarian Lifestyle **123**
   Recognition 123
   Lifestyle Alternatives and Preparations 125
   Location 129
   Densities 130
   Small Rural Towns 131
   Specifications and Philosophy Preferred Land Characteristics 132
   Desirable Infrastructure Project Development Features 133
   Homes **136**
   Design Philosophy Specifications 136
   Empowerment of the Country Business 138
   Relational Enterprises **140**
   The Aquaculture Vineyard and Winery 140
   Co-Op Residential Farms 145

10. **Aracadian Village Communities** **148**
    The Village 150
    Population Density 154
    Alternative Energy Resources 155
    Food 156
    Local Geomorphologies 157
    Architecture 158

Building Codes   160
Steel Buildings   161
An Ideal Storage and Survival Solution   162

11. Alternative Locations   **165**

12. Economic Security Regions   **172**
Things critical to manufacturing survival in
    the coming conditions   **175**
Alternative Energy Resources   175
Reduction in corporate overhead and operating costs   176
Reducing medical costs by hiring a company doctor   176
Eliminate unions that constantly push for higher wages until
    the company is bankrupted by those wages   177

13. Investing for Security and the New World   **179**

14. Religion and Affirmations   **188**

15. Pillars of Wisdom   **193**

Afterward: Noa Ville 2300   **197**

Appendix: Quick Survival Guide to the End of
    The Fossil Fuel World   **203**

Foreword

Unlike many books about the future, this is not the result of divine revelation or mystical enlightenment; it is the result of careful research. Unfortunately, it's possible to predict the future with a high degree of accuracy if the predictions are based on evolving existing conditions unlikely to realize mitigating factors.

Before the 1979 oil shortages, and before the recent California blackouts, there was little public warning or awareness. Both cases were the result of manipulation or bad management by people we invested with a degree of trust. Fortunately both events were repaired and life returned to normality.

Unfortunately, they were warnings concerning arriving conditions for which there may be no ideal solutions. It's unlikely the arriving similar events can be fixed in a comprehensive manner after they occur, because the causes are so foundational. We need fossil fuels to create the infrastructure and alternatives before the fossil fuels begin their serious decline. The hope of mitigation lies in realizing the truth prior to the event and beginning a concerted effort to cure the problems before they occur in their darkest forms.

Maybe there will be more oil and gas discoveries than expected, new fields will come on line more quickly, conservation and market factors will work, and new alternative technologies will be realized and deployed faster than expected. Unfortunately it's more likely the carefully and expensively realized expected factors will arrive than that the unexpected will magically occur.

We will not run out of fossil fuels tomorrow, however, in a few years at most, demand will exceed supply more or less permanently, as a result there will be critical shortfalls of energy, particularly in the cities, and since fossil

9

fuels are foundational, every aspect of society will endure a critical inflationary curve that will likely include spikes and dips. This condition may result in a worldwide depression, a depression greater than any in history.

The purpose of this book is to demonstrate the imminent problems and hopefully help people realize that at every level of society, they are responsible for conditions leading towards their own demise. It's also reasonable to assume we will not fix the full set of problems in time, so the book offers sensible alternatives and preparations in anticipation. At this time, it has become incumbent upon all persons of stature in related fields to step up and educate the public with the truth, and to begin making contributions towards the alternatives that lead towards mitigation.

This book has been written in a popular style designed to be readable; to make a number of points quickly, and demonstrate there may be ways to work towards avoidance. The scholarly material is out there in other forms if you need verification, and you are encouraged to do your own more detailed research. The Author strongly suggests you start with 'www.oilendgame.org' the book you will find there, which is (as this is written) downloadable for free, is a comprehensive and scholarly look at the issues in a positive light. Then go to 'www.oilcrash.com' for a more forceful interpretation of the issues. In the Author's opinion much of the material in the first site is too optimistic; some of it based on wrong or false assumptions and pathways that will never yield hoped for solutions, while the material on the second site is in a few ways overly pessimistic and fails to offer real solutions. The truth will most likely be better than the oil crash material, but worse than the projections in the 'Oil End Game', as the issues are not going to conveniently wait until 2025 for everyone to make the transition, and it is unlikely everyone will perform as suggested. Keep in mind that books like 'The Oil End Game" are dangerous as they make it appear somebody else will take care of the issues for us so we don't have to do anything personally, other than mindlessly continuing to squander our future.

In the end analysis the future will unfold in unexpected ways. Nothing in this material should be taken as ultimate truth, in future projections such things are impossible. Nevertheless prudence and wisdom dictate an informed decision is better than one based on ignorance, and it's a certainty that if we do nothing towards solving the fossil fuel issues, we as a race are in for some very troubled times.

Part One

Conditions

"What people need to hear loud and clear is that we're running out of energy in America."
President George W. Bush 2001

Chapter One
Yesterday and Today

Chief Nik'e Temaru slowly lowered his old body onto the stone chair, grumbling about the need for some cushions, while the children gathered about the evening's fire, waiting. A bronze skinned woman brought him a steaming cup of crushed lemon leaf tea. Too stiff to bend down and place it with the ceremony it deserved, he reached into his shirt pocket and quietly dropped a small pebble of polished coral, to join the others about his feet. "IOraNa; it was your great great great grandfather Oscar Great Chief that brought the end of corruption and oppression to the islands and our peoples. But Oscar did a lot more, he brought back the good things of our ancient Arioi ways, listened to the forest and the sea, and used wisdom to bring the technologies of the howlie's power and their other things to the islands, the things that have allowed us to live in comfort in Rohutu Noa Noa, through the howlie's end times."

Headlines

1997: Tourists on adventure cruise discover the ice has melted across wide areas of the polar cap, making it difficult to play golf on the North Pole.

1997: Greenland ice core study projects yield evidence ice age climate rollovers have occurred within a ten-year period; that such events are directly preceded by global warming caused by greenhouse gasses.

1997: Scientific American publishes theory indicating cause of last ice age may have been melting of ice dam at Hudson Bay, upsetting function of the Greenland Sink, a mechanism that drives the North Atlantic Current, which brings warm south Atlantic waters north, allowing prevailing wind patterns to warm Europe and make it habitable.

1998: Research identifies likely cause of last ice age as massive fresh water melt and rain loading of the Greenland Sink, but ads sources such as glacial and iceberg melt water, including large contributions from Northern Europe, Greenland Ice Sheet and Russia.

1999: Evidence derived from tritium and helium isotope satellite tracking of ocean currents indicates Greenland Sink and North Atlantic current has reduced normal flow by one third between 1980 and 1999. Academic studies had not expected this level of impact for at least another hundred years.

June 2001: Significant snow falls in London in June, midst a summer of cold and rainy weather.

2001: Global Oil use approaches 30 Billion Barrels per year: Petrol industry paper indicates fuel price escalation and shortages from 2004 onward.

2001: President Bush orders massive bulk purchase and storage of crude, for national security:

2001: Studies indicate 70% of the worlds remaining oil reserves reside in Middle East:

2001: U.S. President begins seeking a national referendum towards a massive first strike of Iraq, ostensibly to dethrone Saddam Hussein and destroy his weapons of mass destruction, more likely to achieve stability in the region, and greater control over oil. Iraq retains second largest oil reserves in the world, and possibly the largest and cheapest to recover.

Spring 2002: NOAA indicates presence of a new El Nino forming in the south eastern Pacific several years earlier than normal cycle:

Spring 2002: Further indications Greenland Sink is in process of stopping.

Summer 2002: Study of Alaskan Glaciers indicates massive acceleration of melt rate calculated at 24 cubic miles per year for 2002. Similar glacial melt conditions are accelerating worldwide: Academic and super computer weather models are unable to explain this level of accelerated melting as a result of global warming data alone.

Summer 2002: Long term studies indicate world wide sea level rise of 8" since 1960: Other studies indicate massive escalation of breakup of Antarctic ice shelves leading to speculation on collapse conditions for the nearly three mile thick Antarctic ice cap. Simultaneous research indicates critical conditions in the Greenland Ice Cap. Research indicates melting of all worlds' ice would yield sea level rise of 100 meters, and inundate coastal and lowland areas home to 2/3 of the world's population.

Summer 2002: Low-lying communities across Greenland inundated by ice sheet melting, commence process of wholesale relocation.

Summer 2002: Massive rains, glacial melt and floods raise level of Black Sea by 16" in one month: Northern Europe ravaged by record flooding. India suffers huge record monsoon rains. In China, the Yangtze and other tributaries flood a massive system of lakes causing the evacuation of millions of people in nearby cities. In Bangladesh hundreds of thousands of homes are destroyed and millions displaced, all of this barely makes the news on CNN.

Summer 2002: Massive glacier in southern Russia breaks apart, huge chunk slides fifteen miles buries village and kills 130 people

Fall 2002: Sudden onset of hurricanes in south Atlantic. Theory is published indicating collapse of the Greenland Sink does not allow progress of heated South Atlantic water north, as a result waters in the hurricane belt are significantly heated and hurricanes grow larger more powerful and numerous.

August 2002: Massive meeting of the U.N Earth Charter organization in Johannesburg South Africa. Participants talk about the value of solar cookers and other minor technologies, but fail to use the opportunity to address the critical issues.

2002-2003: Several parties realize the end of the fossil fuel based world society is in sight, that governments and major corporations around the planet have been hiding this truth, and frustrating efforts by the G77 and numerous private concerns to initiate the alternative energy programs needed. Several web sites are published offering concurrent theories, statistics and implication sets.

Early 2004: Crude prices reach benchmark of $30.00 a barrel, and stabilize near that point for a couple of months. Consumers begin to complain about rising prices at the pump, but analysts say that unlike past fuel price rises this time it's not likely to go down again.

Summer 2004: Thousands killed and millions displaced across India and Bangladesh by horrendous Monsoons.

Mid 2004: Crude prices jump to record $50.00 per barrel, as world consumption approaches 1.3 trillion gallons per year.

Late Summer 2004: As theory predicted two years earlier, hurricanes stack up across the unnaturally warm Mid Atlantic, causing massive damage.

September 2004: Study indicates North Polar ice cap is melting four times faster than previously predicted, partly because surface areas exposed from snow and ice melt absorb substantially more heat. Study also indicates massive areas of permafrost melting are releasing huge amounts of methane and CO2 into the atmosphere.

September 2004: While people in the U.S. concentrate on hurricanes, no one seems to notice that so far in 2004 the Eastern Pacific has suffered the worst typhoon season in recorded history. Including truly massive super-typhoons that do not make landfall and therefore do not receive much news coverage.

September 2004: Oil Company advertising campaign. A young lady says; "The world is running out of oil, we are Americas largest supplier of natural gas, and its largest operator of solar farms." In another commercial, " The world cannot transition from an economy heavily dependent on oil without an alternative, natural gas is the alternative and the oil companies will be there to provide it." At the same time Europe is expecting an economic depression in the approaching winter as a result of a huge spike in natural gas prices, which are being blamed on the sudden depletion of natural gas yields from the North Sea platforms, largely operated by the same oil company. To anyone who understands the full implications, these commercials are utterly chilling.

October 2004: Despite warnings of bankruptcy by virtually all members of the American independent trucking industry, a projected 30% increase in home heating oil for the winter, and a firm oil price now at $53.00 per barrel, both John Kerry and President George W. Bush steadfastly refuse to address the energy problem in their respective campaigns. Why? Because both know it is not politically expedient to address a problem which is only going to get worse, and for which there is no full solution… It has already begun.

We are at war. It is a war unprecedented in history. Billions of lives may be destroyed, the world we have known may end. The enemy we face is the most prolific ruthless intelligent powerful and unforgiving foe of all. We have met that enemy; it is us.

This war is about survival on this planet. There are now over 6.4 billion souls on the Island Planet living on a razor's edge between social continuity and catastrophe. By 2050 that number may rise to Eleven Billion. This is a fearsome thought, and by the time you finish this book you will know with certainty why this war is *not* about other people living in other places.

The greatest weapons of survival and security in this war will be anticipation and acceptance, appropriate action, wisdom and technology. The most important strategic directives for self-defense will be personal responsibility, creative intelligence, location, co-operation, community, sustainable self-sufficiency, political stability, appropriate infrastructure, careful conservation, manipulation of essential resources, and most important of all, enlightenment of the enemy, us.

It's possible that large-scale pervasive changes in the morphologies of human conduct, or new discoveries in the field of energy may push the advent of full-scale war slightly further into the future than this book predicts, but unless there is a major technological miracle, the truth is this war is inevitable and the first battles have already begun. Do your own research, arrive at your own conclusions, consider your personal conditions and goals, but whatever you do, wake up, get your head out of the sand and look around, this stuff is real, it's happening now, it is our future.

Across history our goal has been to overcome the vicissitudes of nature and create conditions of comfort and security in the midst of an unforgiving environment. In the past the effects were localized, now they are merging to become global. We face a mandatory shift in the ways we approach our relationship with nature. The entire planet is now our home in the unforgiving oceans of space.

Nature has been kind across our history, but nature can be cruel on a global scale. As a result, we must make a shift towards responsibility and learn to live within the constraints of nature in a cooperative way. This is a war we cannot win; the best we can hope for is sustainable peace. The enemy is us first, then the loss of abundant energy, then climate, then environmental destruction at all levels. Our Planet reached its maximum long term sustainable population of humans fifty years ago, but foolishness and resourcefulness combined with the gift of fossil fuels made us blind to the fact, now we have little time left in which to take the steps needed to insure at least some survival and social continuity, we must act now, or suffer the consequences.

The Earth is a small near-perfect island, trapped in a sea of desolation called space. Space is an ocean of nothing so huge and empty it staggers our imagining. This is our *only* island, it has been the story of our origins and our life for four *billion* years, and even if we succeed in crossing the great sea and finding a new home, the earth will remain the distant long lost paradise of the human race, for the remaining four billion years of our star.

Unfortunately there's no royal catamaran we can build in the foreseeable future that will take us on to the next island. It's possible but highly uncertain that time may yield a means to accomplish this task, but if we are to find a viable interstellar technology we must first survive the arriving future with a sophisticated and functioning world society.

Chief Temaru stopped to catch his breath, wistful melancholy in his heart, as he slowly worked his way up the wide path towards the Cliff of the Winds. He crooked his neck at the now silent and rusted columns of the great old Howlie wind turbines that stood sentinel, staring blankly out to sea with endless expectation like the great Moa of the Ancients on Rapa Nui. Then smiled quietly as the breeze stiffened and the smaller turbines on the log towers began their almost sacred whisperings in the wind.

"Too many" He thought to himself; "Too many on Tai'iti Nui, what to do? What to do?"

Chapter Two
Too Many

Eleven Billion people in forty-four years, the construction of 8 new cities the size of Greater Los Angeles every year for the next 44 years, 352 new mega-metropolises. Will they be sparkling new economic powerhouses like the new cities of China, or the dramatic Arcotropic mega hives once envisioned by Paolo Soleri? No. The reality is most of these new populations will attach to the outskirts of existing cities in the form of massive, intensely populated slums and badly built high-rises. Sao Paulo Brazil and Mexico City are the future. Most of these populations will be low income, meaning little or no tax basis that can be directed at infrastructure improvement.

This mega growth around existing cities will cripple and gridlock the metropolitan cores, producing pollution, disease, and squalor at a level unknown since medieval London during the Black Plague. This new constantly meta-growing population will consume natural resources at a hypoxic rate, stripping the forests, sucking up the fresh water, precious oil and coal like a great sponge, destroying the worlds fisheries, causing the extinction of most of the world's competitive animal species. There is no way to gloss over this single driving fact, *all of mankind's problems on the Earth ultimately and fundamentally reside in a single condition called overpopulation.*

It's hard to define the ideal human population on this planet, but a reasonable long-term healthy sustainable figure, in the context of modern technology and learning is around four billion or less.

In much of the world the available implementation of birth control has been severely constrained by outdated dogma of certain religious institutions, particularly the Catholic Church. Catholic Christianity was deployed across the world in part because it was empowered by the most sophisticated technologies of warfare during the time of exploration and conquest, and the outdated mandates of it's creed will cause ever increasing suffering.

Most of the great religions come to us out of different times and different worlds, what was right in the eyes of the great teachers during their lives, might not be right for the world as it is now. Regarding social conduct, all of the great spiritual teachers have simply stated in many different ways that every human being carries an inherent personal mandate to act responsibly. Acting responsibly means the intentional avoidance of betrayal. In today's world the greatest responsibility each of us carries is to reduce the size of our families. Why? Because if we don't we will most certainly betray the future existence of the race.

The real reason churches and governments encourage population growth has nothing to do with moral imperatives, but instead with the economics of institutions that are socially parasitic. In order for religious institutions to go on building marble cathedrals and Mosques, and keep their Bishops in stretch limousines, and some of their Mullah's in falsely inspired Jihads, or for bureaucrats to increase their power base and personal incomes, the populations they receive their tithes and taxes from, must continue to grow.

All of the great souls whose teachings founded the worlds great religions lived their lives simply and humbly, and the fathers of both ancient and modern democracy were intelligent farmers who founded their institutions in reaction to oppressive governments designed to serve the needs of those in charge of government, at the expense of the people those governments were supposed to serve.

Now the perverse unenlightened policies of church and state have yielded a world on the brink of self-destruction, a general condition that fails to serve the purposes of church, state, or society. Therefore it's past time for a reevaluation of all policies that encourage population growth.

Birth control methods exist and are effective, and humans will have sex. Without a full and pervasive deployment and educational program that teaches the methods, technologies, and alternatives, in combination with the health and moral imperatives of responsible conduct, the future history of the human race will be severely undermined.

The realization of overpopulation issues is nothing new, the entire nature of the problem was first addressed in 1798 and more comprehensively in 1803 in a paper called 'The Principles of Population' by Thomas R. Malthus. Malthus predicted that the population of a region would always grow until checked by famine pestilence or war, and that even if agricultural production were improved, the net result would be an increase in population, and the general welfare of the people that agriculture served would not improve.

Times have changed since Malthus, and the agricultural regions that formed the context of his paper have come together to form a single region called Earth, but in all other ways the predictions and morphologies he expressed 200 years ago have come to pass in a very big way. Technology, energy and careful politics have allowed us to push back the pervasive effects of pestilence famine and war sufficiently to allow the world's population to grow well beyond the point of catastrophic collapse ultimately predicted by Malthus. In doing so they have allowed us to assume the false attitude that we will be able to overcome all the problems we create, they have allowed us to ignore the most basic and fundamental problem of all successful living species, overpopulation.

Make no mistake we are at war with ourselves, *we,* are the disease reeking havoc on the earth. We are consuming the gifts of the earth at a rate equivalent in all ways to a third stage terminal cancer. Successful diseases are never those that kill their host, they are instead self-moderating and chronic in nature. We must heal the whole being, or all of us will certainly die.

Religion's Role and Responsibility:

Reconsider the now inappropriate mandates of the world's antiquated religions and moralities. Aside from the enforced and often misguided mandates and policies of governments, and economists, the world's religions are the most powerful social engineering vehicles of the human condition. All of these great religions were the result of teachings of truly great individuals, but they lived in different times and worlds, and much of what they taught has become inappropriate or corrupted by lesser men. The mandates of social survival no longer demand the largest possible family, tribe, or nation. In today's world there is only one tribe. The survival of that tribe now hinges on controlling its size. It has become an issue of lesser evils. Clearly it's less of an evil to prevent a life that has yet to exist than it is to bring that soul into a life of misery. The religions must recognize the hard truth of today's world, and adopt policies of personal responsibility' which now include at the highest levels of ethical morality a reduction in family size.

Change government policies that encourage large families

Fewer children must come to *equal greater wealth* for the family. Individuals who have no children should not be penalized by tax structures while those who do are rewarded. Those living in poverty must be terrified by the prospect of pregnancy before it occurs so that they will have a real incentive to act responsibly. But when unwanted pregnancy occurs, and it will, abortion must be available with the easiest possible venues at the earliest possible date. Abortion is an evil, but less of an evil than unwanted pregnancies or pregnancies that will bring a life of misery to parents children and society. The less stigma and guilt attached to abortion the more quickly such acts will occur, and the quicker the act is accomplished the less of an evil it becomes. China recognized the problem some years ago and sought to forcefully engineer small family size, as did India. Both countries were wrongly condemned by the world community for having foresight and attempting to do the necessary and responsible thing. Admittedly there were abuses, involuntary and arbitrary sterilization of innocent men, and infanticide of females are not answers anyone can accept, but teaching mandating and providing the means with forgiveness and responsibility is, and it's critically important now.

In today's economic conditions, more people are not the answer to general wealth and stability, outdated polices and systems of government that rely on and encourage an ever-growing population must be reconsidered and changed.

Something caught his eye, and he turned to look out to sea. "Yes, it was certain" Tan sails of a large ship breasted the horizon; it would be heading for the quay at Papea'ete. He grumbled to himself as he gave up the hill and sat down on the edge of the path, took that irritating little pest out of his pocket and called his chief of security at the Commune de Faa'a. "IOraNa, Ben, there's a ship coming into Papea'ete, gather the men to meet it, and send a car to collect me, at the Rue De La Vent."

Chapter Three
Today and Tomorrow

The future carries a certainty; the normal life all of us have known for the last one hundred years is quickly coming to an end. Fossil fuels, a gift of the earth, provided the energy needed to build modern society, and it's that same abundant energy that allowed unrestricted growth, until we have reached a population way beyond the boundaries of catastrophic collapse.

For fifty years those of us born into the developed world have enjoyed lives of fantasy made possible by fossil fuels, while the rest of the world lived a distant outland existence barely removed from basic survival. Suddenly, in the last ten years a huge block of the under-developed world has entered the developed world's economic realm, and with that entry has achieved the economic resources needed to convert to consumer societies.

This is a positive realization for the human race. There is no ethical, moral or philosophical imperative that justifies one mans life of wealth against another's life of misery simply because of accidents of birth. Nevertheless, fossil fuels are a limited resource and the sudden advent of three billion new souls acquiring cars and trucks, warmed and cooled homes, televisions computers and the wealth of food that can only be achieved by a fossil fuel based agriculture, combined with the fact that the world's maximum production capacity of oil was reached near the turn of the 21'st century means with certainty, that the end of the fossil fuel based world economy is now arriving with unexpected speed and consequence.

What does this mean? Barring a highly unlikely miracle of technology capable of affecting all the necessary venues of energy use in a massively positive way, or the advent of a world-killing comet, nuclear war, super volcano, or a plague beyond all biblical proportions, the following *will* occur. Energy costs to all users will increase at a rate significantly higher than normal inflation. A few nations will enjoy a short period of new wealth but then an inevitable decline in social structures will begin that will affect everyone on the planet. This decline will continue for a short period in a reasonably civilized fashion until it becomes clear to everyone that energy resources are the foundation of all national securities. Then the energy wars will commence without subtlety of any kind. The resultant taking of energy resources by force will result in massive shortfalls of energy to the losing nations, which will in turn result in social collapse and famines on scales previously unknown in history.

In a nutshell

• **Oil resource discovery peaked in 1962 and has been declining ever since. We've been using huge old fields.**
• **80% of current production comes from fields discovered prior to 1973. The world is currently burning four barrels for every one found.**
• **Industry experts believe 90% of the fields that can be found have been found.**
• **Nearly the entire world's production capacity of oil was pumping in late summer 2004.**
• **In 2003 China's demand for oil increased by 40%, in 2004, 37%, while world wide demand jumped by 32%.**
• **Even if Iraq's production was increased to it's maximum capacity and the remaining Alaskan fields were brought into production instantly. World demand for oil will permanently exceed all possible production by the end of 2006.**
• **The world's demand for Natural Gas is expected to permanently exceed capacity one year later in 2007**
• **In the U.S. natural gas supplies are already on the decline and industry has initiated a massive new infrastructure program for importation.**
• **In the best possible scenario, electrical supply companies will begin intentional nightly blackouts to most cities by early 2008, along with enforced restrictions on air conditioning and heating, by 2009 long-term full blackouts will be common.**

- Total world oil reserves have been systematically overstated by Oil Companies seeking higher stock valuations, and Producer Nations seeking to encourage greater use, and empower their role in the game. As this book is going to press a variety of credible agencies have begun to report that world oil reserves have been overstated by as much as 80%, meaning many of the predictions in this book are unfortunately overly conservative.
- Recently oil prices were kept low in the U.S. by new technologies realized to harvest huge Canadian Oil Sands deposits, which are now the single largest U.S. source of imported oil. However rapidly increasing demand in other parts of the world offset this unexpected windfall, almost as soon as it came online.
- Reserves in the Canadian oil sands and similar deposits, like the massive bitumen fields of Venezuela, and the oil shales of the U.S. are for all practical purposes massively overstated, because of absolute physical and economic constraints, which drastically limit the percentage of the fields that can be recovered.
- By 2009 at the latest, as a result of depleting reserves and decline of discoveries, total oil production will begin a consistent decline of 3% per year, while demand will continue to increase.
- There is no full alternative, and no point in the future when this condition will correct in any positive way. Oil is a finite resource it takes millions of years to create naturally. Again, there is no known solution, no known adequate alternatives. This process is already beginning; it is a certainty it will only get worse.
- By 2010 if population growth continues unrestrained, the cost of fossil fuel based agriculture will exceed 60% of the world's ability to pay for it. Lack of fossil fuel fertilizer support will cause massive crop failures by 2013 or sooner. Many productive areas will be subject to desertification. The famine will be magnitudes of scale greater than any in history.
- Wars of Energy Imperialism will occur. These will not be limited to producing nations but will most likely involve the entire planet.
- By about 2015 this orgy of catastrophic conditions will likely result in a population decline on the order of Billions of people. Unless we take massive steps towards mitigation now, most of the planet's human

infrastructure will also be destroyed, along with most of its ability to pump the remaining oil.
- **Recovery towards any condition resembling world civilization, if it is possible will take at least fifty years, but more likely nearly two hundred.**

In the near term future, as fossil fuel use escalates, newly rich populations and old users, will not allow their governments to restrict energy use beyond a certain level, physical restrictions on petroleum use demanded by a world production already beyond maximum capacity, will result in massive short-term recourse to coal and natural gas. The resultant Carbon Dioxide loadings when combined with ever increasing levels of methane production from agriculture and human populations will result in a spike in greenhouse gas loading of the earth's atmosphere, these levels are already higher than they have been in 430,000 years, but before the fossil fuel orgy is over the effects of those levels may exceed any human hope of correction, and likely result in thoroughly catastrophic conditions. *This will all occur, within the next 30 years.*

It's a fact that large alternative fossil fuel resources do exist in the U.S., which can be processed to yield replacements for oil imports, most notably oil shales, coal, coal culm, and methane hydrates, but they are of little value towards solving the coming oil crises, until somebody does the hard work of bringing them on line.

It's a fact that many fossil fuel pundits argued the Canadians were crazy to try recovering the oil sands. Fortunately a few Canadians failed to listen and proved a viable process that quickly became the single largest source of income for Canada. The same situation currently exists in the U.S., at $50 a barrel; technologies already exist, which make mining of oil shales, and conversion of coal and coal culm (lignite) into petroleum fuels feasible and economically viable now. It's also a fact that enough natural gas lies trapped in Methane Hydrates on the continental shelf of U.S territorial waters off the East Coast to supply current U.S. needs for two hundred years. While the technology to mine the Hydrate resource does not currently exist, it is a certainty it will never exist until appropriate agencies make a concerted effort to develop this critical technology. It's also a fact that technologies exist now capable of doubling gas mileage of all private vehicles in the U.S. This conversion could cut total U.S. oil consumption by 1/3rd. Again somebody has to do it and everybody has to buy into it.

Given current conditions and the obvious consequences of doing nothing, it is without question a fact that the auto manufacturers, the political leaders of the U.S. and nearly all the consumer citizens of the country are currently committing criminal negligence against themselves and the future of their countrymen by not immediately adapting wide sweeping reforms and policies designed to develop and conserve the fossil fuel resource alternatives now. This is because it is also a fact that the effort needed to develop and install these resources at a level that will show a significant effect on overall oil use will take a national effort larger than any undertaken in U.S. history, and will take years to implement and install. It's again a fact that the U.S is looking at serious economic problems from oil shortfalls beginning as this is written (2004) which will likely become economically devastating by 2006.

In the face of this reality America is following one of the most insane possible national economic and general management policies possible. On the one hand we are refusing to make any serious attempt to solve our internal energy shortfalls, as a result a huge chunk of our gross domestic product is being transferred to oil exporting nations. At the same time we are now pursuing a mad dash of corporate irresponsibility in which every possible American job of any real productive impact is being outsourced to cheaper labor in the developing world, while we as consumers are addicted to purchasing cheap imported goods and throwing them away at the first sign of wear. These actions dramatically enhance the economies of the developing world with the disposable income needed to compete with us in our insatiable energy habit, thus increasing dramatically both the worlds' total consumption of fuel, and the price we have to pay for it. We are cutting our own throats in the process. Currently for every dollar America receives from the rest of the planet, four are paid out. While at the same time we are paying huge sums, with legitimate support from no one else, to act as the world's solitary policeman. All this has been going on now for years, and nobody at a personal corporate or national level regardless of substance or size can do business successfully in this fashion and survive.

Unfortunately the fossil fuel resource supply problem, and related self destructive American policies, while the most immediate issues, are not the sum of the problems we face. It's a fact that immediate actions taken to assist the energy supply problem will only buy time, and that if we are to survive the long term, we must find complete non-fossil alternatives. However, because we have been negligent, we need the time that can only be provided by advantaging these alternative fossil resources now.

Again, unfortunately, the massive use of fossil fuels is a double-edged sword, which presents us with another set of problems likely to be equally as hard to overcome.

Our people were lucky, we never had much of anything but the sea and the forest, nothing much to change, in Oscar's time there were all those cars on the circle island road? But, nobody really liked them, the whole island stank of diesel, just foolishness, better gone." The ship was dropping its sails as they drove the rare solar car off the once proud freeway and entered Papea'ete, near the quay. Chief Nik'e had seen pictures of the grand cruise ships that had tied up at the edge of the park; he liked the rare clippers a great deal more. Especially this one, which he now recognized as the Pacific Maranatha Maru, it would be on it's run North from New Zealand to Hawaii, then on to what was left of Japan before its return South, most likely had a hold full of salt mutton. The chief realized he'd forgotten to eat breakfast again; he was looking forward to lunch on board.

Large Scale Environmental Effects of Fossil Fuel Usage

Over the last two hundred years, almost exclusively as a result of human activities, the CO_2 content of the atmosphere has risen by 31% and the methane content by 151%. Methane is twenty times more effective as a green house gas than CO_2. Fortunately its total percentage of the atmosphere is much lower, but it's quickly becoming an important element in climate change.

Most of the current computer model studies of future climate change use a conservative 'forcing' figure of 1% per year compounded CO_2 loading yielding an atmospheric doubling of CO_2 over the next 70 years. This yields conservative predictions of an average global increase in temperature of 1.5 to 6.5 degrees Fahrenheit before the next century. This might sound manageable until you consider that all our activities to date have created a one degree confirmed average rise, and that has been enough to irreversibly commence the melting of the glaciers and the poles, change the weather across the planet, and endanger the Thermohaline engines that drive the ocean currents, which make Europe and much of the Northern Hemisphere habitable. Further, these scientific consensus figures are probably too conservative, as they do not anticipate the sudden economic growth occurring in the developing nations across the globe and the resultant additional spike in loadings that will follow. What is certain is that greenhouse gases, once in the atmosphere do not dissipate or become naturally re-sequestered in the earth and oceans for a very long time and what we are doing now will be almost impossible to fix along timelines that will do any human societies any good.

Careful research conducted on the Greenland Ice sheet indicates that spikes in atmospheric greenhouse gas loading have often preceded previous ice ages. These spikes were likely produced by volcanic activity and or asteroid-comet impacts causing worldwide forest fires. The resultant global warming causes massive fresh water loading of the oceans at critical locations particularly in an area south of Greenland known as the Greenland Sink, and sometimes short-term sea level rising, then the Thermohaline engine of the North Atlantic Current stops functioning normally. This event reduces or nearly stops warm equatorial waters from reaching the North Atlantic causing a massive and sudden change in global climate that may result in the advent of ice ages.

Current computer modeling and general scientific consensus indicates that if the North Atlantic Current does stop, the effects will only be regional, primarily affecting Europe and England with possible reductions in average temperatures of between 14 and 29 degrees Fahrenheit and that these must be superimposed over general global warming figures of between 1.5 and 6.5 degrees Fahrenheit predicted to occur over the next century. This means the climate in England and Europe all the way down to southern France will be the same as the climate in far northern Canada, in other words forty to fifty degrees below zero in the winters, permafrost and very short summers, which in turn means general agriculture and human habitation in these areas will be almost impossible, and certainly impossible for much of Russia and Scandinavia. It is also a fact that even though the general scientific consensus currently indicates no actual ice age will occur, there are significant conflicts in the studies and the very real possibility they could be wrong. Ice age or not, if the Atlantic current stops, the effects will be quickly felt across the planet in social, economic, and military terms.

Of course if this event does occur, it is a given that an additional spike in CO2 loading, and fossil fuel use will occur as a result of what will become absolutely critical new heating and energy use demands across most of Europe and Northern Asia.

That the U.S government takes this issue seriously is reflected in the fact that the CIA and military agencies have already funded major studies concerning the expected impacts and are now using these scenarios in futures planning. Unfortunately none of this research seems to have affected civilian governmental policies, most likely because of private interest lobbying (fossil fuel industries and OPEC nations) and avoidance of negative political perceptions.

Further, planetary greenhouse gas levels are already higher than those recorded prior to many previous ice age roll over events, and these climactic rollover events have and can occur in a period of less than ten years. (Right now atmospheric CO2 is at the highest level in 430,000 years, in that time four ice ages have come and gone) Sea surface sampling and satellite tracking of the critical currents indicates the Atlantic Current failure process is already well underway. However, some factors in the current situation are markedly different. In past rollovers there has been little or no effect to conditions on Antarctica, however it's clear that our activities are in the process of creating a general meltdown at the South Pole as well as at the North. If the ice age rollover does not occur and the North Atlantic current does not completely stop, and atmospheric warming continues, it remains a possibility that a previously unseen environmental condition may occur in which all world ice caps melt. Resulting in a sea level rise across the planet of up to 340 vertical feet, and possibly an unstoppable cycle of ever increasing warming.

Any of these futures will reduce human populations and their impacts on the biosphere. It is a near certainty that one or more of these conditions will occur. Is there anything we can do to stop these futures from unfolding? Probably not. Human nature, socio-political-economic habits, inertia and the purified mandates of survival at all levels indicate that for perhaps the next twenty years governments and economically driven systems will attempt to maintain status quos with Band-Aids. These Band-Aids include ramping up coal and natural gas production, probable massive efforts to bring oil sands and shales into production, a sudden rebirth of nuclear breeder reactors, and continued massive deforestation projects. Most of these efforts will occur because they are the path of power and economics preferred by the corporate giants already in power, because they are 'politically expedient', and because they represent the only apparent and immediate options available capable of meeting the needs and demands of exploding human consumer societies. Make no mistake, these band-aids will be critical to buy time and maintain acceptable social conditions. Unfortunately, they will only increase the atmospheric greenhouse gas loading and hasten the onset of catastrophic natural cycle conditions. Even with the best possible conditions all of these efforts combined cannot meet all of the exploding demands for energy resources dictated by the mathematics of consumer population growth indefinitely.

His grumbling paunch now thoroughly satiated by a rare mutton pie, Chief Temaru had accompanied the captain of the Maranatha Maru and a small contingent crew on the ship's sloop over to Moorea on a scavenging search for spare parts. As they came into the spectacular Baie, Nik'e was once again reminded of the need to clean up the mess, but what to do, what to do? In the early days of the 'fall' hundreds of pleasure craft had arrived in Tai'iti, most were diesel powered mega yachts, and since there was practically no diesel left in the Polynesia at that time most had been stranded or sequestered in Moorea Bay, and had never left. It was policy to let them stay anyway as most of their owners were very wealthy, and the infusion of funds had dramatically bolstered Tai'iti's always-sagging economy at a critical time of transition. Of course Oscar Great Chiefs policy of demanding the larger gensets from many of these vessels as a price of admission, and then refitting them on many of the islands streams turned out to be one of the greatest acts of his illustrious career. But now, after two hundred years of progressive neglect, the once proud multi million dollar vessels were blighting the Baie and something definitely needed to be done. Maybe Martie'n was right, maybe it was time to add them to the reef, but new housing would have to be built, and there would be all that complaining from the residents of the floating community, Nik'e wondered as he did almost everyday why in the hell he let them draft him into being chief, nothing but problems, nothing but problems, maybe next month, maybe the month after, but what a shame, and he knew he would be reminded once again on his return by that exquisite picture of the once virgin Baie that Martie'n had hung on his office wall.

Chapter Four
The Energy Wars

Wars are fought because somebody has something somebody else wants. There are a few alternative reasons, but in the final analysis, they are sophistries of this basic truth. We are consuming our resource wealth at a rate almost beyond comprehension, in a condition called resource financing. We enjoy the lives we enjoy, because we are borrowing from the planet against the future of our race, unfortunately the future has arrived, and the bank is calling in its note. Our energy assets are going bankrupt, and there are no full alternatives. If all oil supplies were shut down tomorrow, within 90 days, much of the world's population would be on the verge of starvation, and witnessing the beginnings of a world war beyond any in history.

Across the planet, except for a single small geographical area, over 70% of all known oil in all possible areas of recovery has already been used. Fully 70% of the planet's remaining oil reserves exist in the Middle East. Within ten years, as the easy oil recovery from virtually every other location begins a serious decline, a condition will arise in which a small number of often less than benevolent individuals will be able to dictate the terms of existence to the rest of the planet, while simultaneously absorbing the lion's share of the planet's wealth.

It's unlikely the governments of power in the world will stand quietly by and allow this state of world ransoming to occur, therefore it is almost inevitable that the world will soon witness a new kind of imperialism, energy imperialism.

Historically the energy market has been self-regulating. If energy prices went up too quickly, people found ways to use less of one type of energy, supply exceeded demand and prices went down. Indeed many of the talking heads on TV are saying somewhat sardonically that we have no oil problem because the inflationary curve beginning in 2004 will result in an economic collapse, which will result in lower demand. In today's massively overpopulated world economy, the potential for economic collapse is not a subject of humor, it is all too real, and worldwide economic collapse now directly translates to historically unseen suffering, famine and death on the order of millions. The path we are following is a very dangerous path. Further, as a result of changing world conditions, the expectation that oil inflation will yield a survivable recession, which will lower demand and self correct the problem is no longer completely valid.

Essentially everyone on the planet, except the U.S. has been used to relatively high, energy prices for a long time. They have built infrastructures and socially engineered their societies accordingly. Most of the countries in the world can absorb raw energy prices that would cause irreparable damage to the U.S. economy, they can afford to pay $100.00 a barrel and survive economically and socially with a few adjustments. Since the U.S. does not own the energy supplies, the supplier nations will sell to whoever can pay their price.

As a result, if lucky, there will be a series of short-term inflation self-correction cycles in the U.S. This will cause a cycling inflationary curve, which will result in a hopefully slow economic meltdown. Unfortunately we now have a world economy. This means when any major nation state undergoes an economic meltdown, a chain reaction will occur, which ultimately brings down all the nation states. Except of course those few nations with an energy export capability. Also recall that the U.S. has a number of non-energy foundational economic arenas that are already seriously over-inflated, these include health care, real estate, and the stock market among others. Any level of inflation seriously undermines these arenas and leads towards collapse, which in turn ripples out quickly in across the board effects.

Less real money in America means Americans will seek to rely even more heavily on cheap imported goods from the developing world, which again increases the developing world's ability to compete for the depleting oil, which increases our cost for energy, and only enhances the inflation of energy costs. The true expected self-correction will not occur in the future we are walking into, it will only be short term cycles that relentlessly lead towards an ultimate shortfall of energy, an ongoing inflation, and ultimately a world wide economic depression from which recovery is effectively impossible.

There are only two alternative pathways that can yield any hope of survival, wars of energy imperialism, and or energy responsibility. Even if successful the first solution only buys time. There is only one permanent solution, energy responsibility through conservation and the massive deployment of energy alternatives that lead towards energy self-sufficiency. We will likely witness the emergence of both alternatives over the next few years. However it is abundantly clear that the ultimate health of the planet and its people now resides entirely in how quickly and how massively world government and economic agencies commence the process of converting to energy responsibility.

Unfortunately, in the modern world economic health is the single largest factor in national securities, and it is very unlikely solutions that lead to energy responsibility can be achieved at the scales needed in time to avert economic disaster. Thus under the banner of national security, it's a near certainty that as economic conditions begin to deteriorate the consumer nations will exercise their military power and take control of the producing nation's resources. This is the reason that right now the OPEC nations are currently pumping at maximum capacity. At this time things are still civilized enough so that strong international diplomacy combined with careful personal assessment of the situation by the producing nations is enough to keep the oil flowing. Of course current U.S. actions in Iraq serve as a powerful warning to producing nations that the U.S. will not hesitate to use its power.

Nevertheless, as demand exceeds supply permanently, diplomacy and supply nation efforts may no longer be enough to maintain the peace. The empowered nations will likely demand the lion's share of the oil, with threat of force initially, and real force as it becomes necessary. If and when this occurs, civil unrest in the producing nations will reduce those nations ability to produce, and total world production will actually fall. When this occurs nation states or alliances of nation states will likely arise which seek to control the resources for their own exclusive use, and as a result the military activities will move from localized oil producing areas until the entire planet is involved.

This will likely be a war unlike any in the past; weapons of mass destruction may be employed without restraint. If it occurs, ultimately, a few *Billion People* will die, and the world's social infrastructures will be destroyed. At the same time the environmental effects of all our fossil fuel use combined with the effects of the warfare will likely become physically intolerable even for the winning nations, if any such thing manages to exist. Is this the future any of us want? Is it necessary? Is it unavoidable?

All democratic governments operate under an inherent mandate of trust and stewardship towards the people they work for. The first order of business is to provide social and economic stability and an acceptable standard of living for all their people, in order to do this, governments must anticipate arriving conditions and define policies accordingly.

Democratic governments are driven by politics. In politics image and the perception of trust and stewardship, along with strength of character and ethical leadership are paramount. Politicians inherit the responsibility to make the hard, unwelcome decisions most likely to yield the best future for their people. If such decisions are made with powerful foresight and conveyed with clarity to the people, they are usually accepted. If hard decisions can be accomplished in such a way that almost no one suffers undo hardship, everyone grows wealthier in the full gambit of the key indices of the quality of life, and their leader's primary mandates are fulfilled.

Unfortunately as this is written a presidential campaign leading to the election of the person who will fill the most powerful position in the world is underway, both candidates and their running mates have blatantly refused to address the looming issues related to energy because both recognize there are no painless solutions, and that the issue is politically not expedient. The actions and mindsets of both of these candidates do not bode well for the future of the planet.

The world currently faces the most powerful set of common foes known to past and future history. Right now that enemy is quietly preparing for war, in a few years time it will attack with ferocity. The battlefield is everywhere across the earth, no land will be immune. Its affects will be greater than the most hideous fears spawned by the imagined nuclear wars of the fifties and sixties, but make no mistake, the threat of nuclear war is still very real in the world, and there will be no greater incentive to use these weapons than the desperate need to acquire energy, or the need to acquire areas of survivable climate in the event of ice age, cooling in the northern hemisphere or other effects of global warming. But nuclear war might only be a small aspect of this new world war.

Biologicals will be the most efficient tools of acquisition. Only a few hundred years ago when the Europeans decided they had a divine right by fiat to own the new world, smallpox, flu and the common cold were their preferred weapons of choice against this authors ancestors. The new genetically engineered plagues resting quietly in the world's military vaults are far more effective and lethal than those were at reducing existing populations and 'cleansing' areas for resettlement or energy acquisition, and they come with built in vaccines for the conquering 'heroes'.

The phrase, 'billions of people may die' is not hyperbole. Keep in mind that since the end of the last great depression almost every single person in America has been outrageously spoiled. We tend to fabricate our general impression of how the rest of the world lives from the movies we watch, we maintain a sort of subtle national impression that everyone in Europe lives on the shores of Lake Como, in mansions, or on vineyard estates in Tuscany, or that the developing world lives in near paradisiacal thatch villages in pleasant jungles or along the sea shore. The truth is 75% of the rest of the world's population, both rich and poor, lives in intensely populated cities in tiny apartments; critically dependent on infrastructures that are largely based on fossil fuel energy subsides for their successful existence. They have learned to make do with a lot less energy than we have, but are in most cases already at the minimum level of energy use needed to sustain them. Any significant economic inflation or shortfall of energy has far more dangerous and critical effects to them than to us. If or when the energy riots begin in those places, the breakdown of social imperatives will be dramatic, pervasive, and ultimately deadly on scales unseen in history.

The United States, almost alone among the nations continues to be the single completely irresponsible energy abuser. At the very least we should have been madly developing our internal alternative energy sources, and developing, manufacturing, and *buying* the highest possible mileage cars, when we received the first warning in 1979, but instead we subjugated our lives and national policies to the best interests of big oil, by telling our politicians big gas guzzling cars, pickups, and SUV's were a divine right and cultural icon of the American citizen. We should have done the right thing, not because we were worried about the end of the world, or because we wanted to be responsible to the rest of the world, or because we were worried about climate change, but for the simple common sense economic health of the nation. Now it may very well be too late.

What will we do when the oil shortages become serious and gasoline hits ten dollars a gallon? As the strongest military in the world, we will arrange conditions that seem to publicly justify the invasion of oil rich countries in the name of freedom and national security, then go and take the oil. Initially, it won't be obvious, the new leaders, out of 'gratitude' to us for 'liberating' their nations will sell us huge quantities of their precious oil quietly at a discount compared to what the rest of the world would be willing to pay. (As this is written the nation of Chad in Africa is suing the developer of its oil fields for selling its oil way below the world market to preferred customers, for reasons of political expediency, and or corrupt re-selling practices, this is not the only case or the last case.) Maybe we will only have to do this once, and then follow that event with discrete strong-arm diplomacy. Maybe our leaders saw the looming oil shortage problem in advance and have quietly taken the necessary steps to prepare.

If this sounds like our recent history in Iraq and the Middle East, maybe it is. Nobody is arguing that Sadam was a great guy, or the world isn't better off without him. Fact is Iraq never fully developed it's oil potential, so it's still in the ground; it's nearer to the surface than any other oil on the planet which means it's cheaper to get, and some estimates indicate there may actually be more oil in Iraq than in all the rest of the Middle East combined.

This has a tendency to sound like nefarious manipulation. It could be, and conspiracy pundits have carried it out to it's fullest implications already; but before you blame everything in this book on the White House consider that the previous administration and the administration before it, had full knowledge of all these arriving conditions, and did effectively nothing towards their mitigation. So maybe the current administration is doing the best they can in the most politically expedient way. Will you complain about the Iraq war when gasoline hits $7.00 a gallon and then the Iraqi's start pumping five million barrels a day and the price drops to $3.00 for a while? Would you complain if you fully understood that right now the entire fate of the entire planet resides in the singular hands of the King of Saudi Arabia and no one else?

As a result there is no question that given the arriving oil depletion, and the effects it implies, liberating Iraq and developing it's infrastructure, and oil industry, and installing a friendly government that can be invited into the clique of world management nations may be the best thing for the world right now.

Regardless, even if the best forecasts for Iraqi oil turn out to be true, and it all works out perfectly, Iraq will buy us a few more months of world economic growth than this book indicates. But unless we start the biggest most comprehensive engineering project ever undertaken right now, targeted at installing a world wide alternative energy infrastructure, and installing the necessary conservation measures, those few months or years will simply be a slightly longer garden party before the energy wars that herald the end of modern society.

Does the construction of all this new alternative energy stuff have to represent a burden on societies, absolutely not. Hitler became the most wildly popular leader of mid century Europe, during the last great world depression not because he was a great speaker, (Though that helped) but because he galvanized a depressed population and put them all to work on the largest national infrastructure rebuilding project ever undertaken in Europe. He told them Germany could be a truly great nation once again, not as good as it once was before World War One, but better than it had ever been. He galvanized the pride of the German people and put them to work doing something constructive, they got paid for their work, and the economy magically healed itself. It was only after he got the national projects underway that he turned the German industrial machine he had created towards his own more nefarious agendas. Here in America our President Roosevelt brought us out of the same depression by using many of the same tools.

Unfortunately, America has now become a nation of spoiled paper pushers, overpaid doctors and lawyers, and underpaid hamburger turners. We have given away our real productivity, our manufacturing capability, our honestly earned income venues and the good jobs to the developing world, and have come into fooling ourselves that we can make a living indefinitely by manipulating imaginary money in marginally sophisticated ways, and by simply serving each other, and that corn and wheat and lettuce, and the biggest guns in the world, will be enough to support all the rest of us forever. The truth is that as this book is written we stand at the edge of a new and potentially horrendous depression, greater than any seen in our history.

We don't need to walk ourselves into that. Instead we can put ourselves to work on massive alternative energy projects that yield critically important jobs, pride and healthy genuinely earned incomes to the people that work on them. Every dollar invested in a massive solar farm, yields a virtually endless stream of energy dollars, each of those energy dollars created right here from the sun or from a major hydro facility, means energy that can subsidize productive manufacturing enterprises, those enterprises can be competitive against a lower paid worker in China or India because the cost of energy to the factory in China or India will be much higher in the very near future.

Every solar farm dollar spent here yields five or six back immediately upon completion, but it also keeps on yielding a river of money effectively forever. Why, because initially that dollar stays here and helps our internal economy, it saves several dollars that that would otherwise be sent to the Middle East, it saves totally wasted dollars spent trying to defend ourselves from terrorist's who are financed indirectly by oil, then it allows internal industry that is directly competitive with China, which saves dollars sent to China, which then saves more because China has less dollars to compete with us for the purchase of oil from the Middle East. And, this economic benefit goes on and on like a river flowing and only improves over time, because unlike fossil fuels which will only escalate in real cost, solar farms will not run out of fuel for four billion years.

The idea that we are in a world economy and must co-operate internationally by opening our markets and outsourcing our productivity is not justified by the argument that if we don't then the world will refuse to buy our goods. This is simply wrong. Why? Because the world cannot feed itself across the next fifty years and America is the single most productive agricultural machine in the world. China's wheat regions are literally drying up and their shortfall of grain will be horrendous. India, Central and South America, and Africa cannot possibly find the resources to feed the looming urban mega slums that are the certainty of their futures. In the arriving world, food will be gold, and America will be the world's largest exporter, and the world's savior, but only if the fossil fuels are conserved for agriculture, and only if we maintain economic stability. The only way we can do that is to cure our energy abuses and work towards internal energy sustainability.

We don't need to be galvanized with pride, and we don't have to wait for a world depression to commence rebuilding our national energy infrastructure. Especially because unlike last time, this time there will be no energy to do it with. We can resurrect the American economy before it collapses, by initiating a healthy and responsible national program of energy self-sufficiency now, and the net result will be nothing but good, not just for us but for everyone on the planet.

Our government is fond of starting new agencies whenever there is a perceived need; we've created half a dozen just to deal with the idiot Bin Laden. The energy problem is a whole lot larger and will not be solved by private enterprise working alone, what we need is a new Mega Tennessee Valley Authority, a private agency empowered by government, with government monies and authority, but not limited to a geographical area, or a particular venue. It's mandate will be to look at any venue that can produce energy without using fossil fuels, or fossil fuel alternatives that can replace oil in the near term shortfall, and then, with the full power of the U.S.

government behind it move forward on a near war footing to get those technologies and projects built and functioning at the soonest possible time, at the largest possible scales.

Unfortunately, the sad fact is we probably will not do anything until it is too late, instead we will figure out ways to manipulate the world energy markets so that we can continue to enjoy the cheapest oil on the planet and continue our reckless and abusive life of fantasy right up to the very end. When the wars begin we will act simultaneously surprised, thoroughly justified, and we will cheer on our armies activities against all those other evil people who just want to make a living and share this planet with us. It's a certainty that all those other people out there will not simply sit back while we trash their lives.

These new wars and their extended effects will not kill a few thousand or a few million, they will kill several billion souls, and there will be no true winners, only losers.

In the midst of this unfolding future, at any time, it, the other great enemy, may also arrive as a dramatic and sudden environmental event, or a slow but relentless change in world climates.

The mammoths quick frozen in the beginning of the last ice age, died in the height of the summer, with summer blooms still un-chewed in their mouths, they were frozen solid in a manner of minutes, not by some imaginary physical pole tilt for which there is little evidence, but by a meta storm, that occurred in the midst of a documented spike of atmospheric CO_2.

Even without a meta-storm event, the evidence indicates the North Atlantic Current is stopping. It brings billions upon billions of gallons of warm South Atlantic water north along the coast of England and Europe. It's a fact most Americans seldom realize, but most of Europe is above the 45th parallel, at latitudes equivalent to far northern Canada. European civilization exists because of the North Atlantic Current. At it's current rate of decline the North Atlantic current might entirely cease to exist by 2010. After that the only inhabitable land left in Europe will be south of a line that bisects the Pyrenees and runs the northern coast of the Mediterranean. Most of Europe, Russia and possibly China, Japan Canada and the northern U.S will be frozen.

Most of the world south of that line is already overcrowded, underdeveloped, and except for oil, low in recoverable resources. When it suddenly begins to be fifty below zero in Germany all across the winter, and a hundred below across Russia, and it snows with regularity in London in the summer, where will all those people go? They will go south. Will the overstressed southern nations invite them in with open arms?

In America it is only slightly better, because we will be moving south but still in our own country. But that's not the end of it, when the Atlantic current stops, the warm water stays in the mid Atlantic and generates hurricanes, bigger hurricanes and a lot more of them As this is being written the largest mass evacuation in the history of the United States is underway in Florida in advance of hurricane Francis, and Ivan and Jeanne are right on her heals. Right now we are calling this a typical American adventure, unless of course you happen to be one of those folks in Florida or the Gulf, for whom this stuff is starting to get really tiresome If the current stops fully, historically 2004 will be seen as a slow year for hurricanes, and every following year will see an endless parade of them, some of them huge running all the way up the eastern seaboard until one of the big ones turns into a super storm that makes it all the way to New York. When that happens the twin towers will be a historical hiccup. Eventually all of the eastern seaboard, and the coast of the gulf of Mexico, and all of Florida, all of these areas will have to be turned into national parks, because the only alternative will be national bankruptcy as we continually try to rebuild all these areas over and over and over again.

These are the futures we face; the price we have to pay for the gift of fossil fuels, irresponsible procreation and consumption, the evidence is clear real verifiable and concrete.

So far we continue to sleep in the bliss of ignorance just as we did before Pearl Harbor, while the enemy is massing even now. The chances for victory are already slim, but they remain real. How was the war that began at Pearl Harbor eventually and finally won? Victory was achieved as a result of the most massive and intense single industrial and technological effort ever undertaken by man, it was called the Manhattan Project; its result was peace, achieved through the ultimate expression of terror.

The enemy we now face is unlike any enemy in recorded human history. It will require a Manhattan Project of unprecedented size, the full energies of the most brilliant human minds. But its goal will not be to create the ultimate terror; instead its *goal* can be nothing short of the creation of a long-term paradise for all mankind upon the earth, well into the foreseeable future:

Our world leaders must stand up and lead, admit mistakes, stop serving private interests, make the hard policy decisions best for everyone while there is still time to avoid the worst scenarios.

Politicians, pundits, economists and conservative scientists will decry this content as sensationalist, and unfounded. They will point to discoveries, alternative fossil fuels in reserve, and the historical presence of similar climactic cycles. Here is the good news they will point too. The U.S. does have oil left off the west coast, some in Alaska, some in the Gulf of Mexico. Mexico has recently announced significant new deep-water fields, there are some discoveries along eastern slopes of the Andes, and Columbia is producing a significant contribution, Russia still has some oil in reserve, there are significant deposits under development around the Caspian and Black seas, and Kazakhstan, and then there is the oil in Iraq and of course the rest of the Middle East. There is significant oil left, and the world is not going to run out completely overnight.

So what is really going on? The profits of oil companies and supply nations dramatically increase as demand inflates the retail price, and since environmentalists scream whenever any of the oil companies suggest tapping anything in the U.S. the oil companies and supply nations are content too and actually have an incentive to agree with the environmentalists to a degree. Higher prices also force conservation and result in reduced consumption, which has historically down cycled price escalations.

In addition, the oil companies are not really in the business of looking out for our welfare, or even increasing the amount of energy they and we have available, they are in fact in the business of making money. Virtually all of them have been aware of the arriving conditions discussed in this book for a long time. It costs a lot to look for, find and develop new oil resources, and it has been more than obvious to them for a long time that the opportunities for profitable discovery have been dwindling dramatically. However, they have an obligation to keep their stock prices high, and in the case of oil companies a lot of their stock value resides in the size of their reserves, so in 2003 and 2004 they embarked on a policy set that included mergers, which allows the resulting merged companies to present the illusion that their now combined reserves are larger. Only a couple of them saw the writing on the wall in a more realistic and positive light and began to take a serious look at, and venture into alternative forms of energy production.

Adding fuel to this fire, almost no one fully anticipated the relatively sudden impact of China and India, and the scale of relentless demand growth in America. The world is not going to run out of oil overnight, however, economic factors and actual physical depletion have conspired hand in hand to accelerate the advent of the fossil fuel energy collapse.

If current trends continue, we will see a consistent decline in the supplyside's ability to meet growing demand. As everyone desperately seeks to fill this demand, oil reserves and new discoveries will not be able to keep up, and the problem will only grow worse as time goes on. The following point is critically important. The oil supply does not have to disappear for the predicted effects to occur, it only has to fail to meet demand in a consistent manner over a period of time. Because oil is the single most critical and foundational resource, which has allowed almost every single aspect of the world society we have built to exist, when demand exceeds supply consistently an inflationary spiral will occur across all fields of all economies on the planet. It's this inflationary spiral and its extended implications, combined with the fierce international competition that will arise for the remaining oil resources that will result in the predicted effects.

In concert with this set of problems, there will be climate changes, exactly what those climate changes will be is at this time impossible to predict with comprehensive certainty, but it is a certainty they will occur because they already are occurring. At the very least the nations affected by these climate changes will be required to deal with them economically and this will present a significant added burden on the affected societies at exactly the same time they are required to deal with the effect's of the fossil fuel inflationary spiral.

It is also a fact that dealing with the expected climate changes will dramatically increase demand for fossil fuels beyond the anticipated normal growth projections.

The Energy Fast

It's difficult for an addict to think about life without its addiction(s), and it's a fact that we are addicted to artificially massive amounts of energy in support of our daily lives. Try to imagine a world where no water came out of your faucets, no toilets flushed, no showers at all, a life with no food on supermarket shelves, no way to get to the supermarket except your feet, where it gets dark when the sun goes down. Imagine a life where the temperature inside your house is always the same as the temperature outside your house. Imagine a life without television, computers, cars, trucks, coffee, tea, tobacco, radio, telephones, refrigerator-freezers, streetlights, and all the goods and services we take for granted. Think about these conditions going on not for the typical few hours or days, but for weeks that stretch into months and then years and then effectively forever. Now think about this life in the midst of an ongoing major disaster or war. The onset of winters that are fifty below zero, or a drought that goes on for years. Think about this in the context of a massively overpopulated city; think about it in the context of never ending riots, looting and to use the almost obscene euphemism, social unrest.

You can read this fairly quickly and be done with it, maybe shiver a little at the brutality of the writer. Your gut reaction is that it's a fantasy the writer made up for impact, something false to sell books. The Author lives in a rural area; power outages are a fairly regular occurrence usually fixed in an hour or two by our highly efficient electrical company. However, when they are occurring there is an immediate onset of a kind of tangible nervousness that does not leave until the power returns, a strange kind of almost physically felt boredom coupled with worry and edginess.

These effects are exactly what they seem to be, the actual symptoms of energy addiction withdrawal. Energy withdrawal is not a fun thing, but if this book has so far not made an impact, it might be wise for you to try a little exercise. Try it during a day off, and don't get drastic and do something like turning off the power to your house, as the food in your refrigerator will spoil. Just stop using anything that requires energy that does not come from your body. Think about everything you do before you do it, does it require artificial energy? If it does you are forbidden from doing it; to be effective keep it up for at least twenty-four hours. You are not allowed to make any special preparations, you are not allowed to open the refrigerator door, or go anywhere in your car. Don't be too brutal, drink some warm water from the tap. Think about all of this while you are pursuing your fast. Think about what it really means to have no more artificial energy supporting your daily life, not for a few hours or a few days, but for the rest of your life, for the entire life of your children and grandchildren, and all of the lives of all of the peoples that will follow on this planet forever, because the fossil fuels can never be replaced, ever.

Be certain that you understand the implications of this exercise, and the reality, because it is a certainty that the serious effects of the fossil fuel resource depletion event are beginning economically right now, and will become altogether too physically real in increments, over the next six years.

Make no mistake, we are addicted, and like all true addicts, when our supply is endangered, the normal social constraints we all voluntarily adhere too will disappear. At all social levels, we will do anything and everything necessary to insure the continuing availability of our habit. Altruism, responsible conduct, legalities, worries about murder or international genocide; these things will not even be part of the conversation.

The path we are all walking over those next six years is the most dangerous path we have ever had to walk, it includes the all too real potential for massive world wide economic depression, wars of energy imperialism, population 'cleansing', starvation, famine, pestilence, and the destruction of our environment unlike anything the world has ever seen.

As this is written a group of environmentalists have stopped a company from drilling for natural gas in an area near Glacier National Park. It would be a good idea if those same environmentalists voluntarily stopped using any gas or electricity, or vehicles, because their actions are only hastening the enforced realization of these things upon themselves. It is also a fact that those environmentalists are forcing the U.S. to speed up it's process of buying gas from overseas, that gas has to be liquefied and shipped across oceans, during the process, huge amounts of precious energy are lost in the process of liquefaction and as much as thirty percent of the gas has to be vented directly into the atmosphere during shipping. This is greenhouse gas twenty times more powerful than Carbon Dioxide, and the resultant contribution that they are making will add significantly to the melting of the glaciers in the park they are trying to protect.

The point of all this is that without artificial energy, without fossil fuels, the environmental, personal, and social effects of the meltdown will be far more devastating and occur far more quickly. It is therefore critically important for the environmentalists to realize that right now we need every ounce of fossil fuels we can find in order to accomplish the transition in a civilized manner.

The environmentalists need to realize with absolute clarity; a planet that is hugely overpopulated, economically bankrupt, and seriously energy depleted, is not going to worry about such niceties as environmental impact, the preservation of parks, clean air or water, the deaths of animal species or anything else beyond what has to be done immediately in any way it can be done to insure survival for the next day, the next month and the next year.

Right now we should be drilling in Alaska, off the coast of California, and wherever there is any hope of finding any gas, we should be building huge factories for converting coal to liquid fuels, and we should stop importing coal from overseas and take responsibility for our own energy abuse by opening up and advantaging every possible resource in the U.S. right now, because these things take a long time to do and they cannot be done if the capital is destroyed by an economic depression that is currently starring us in the face.

Simultaneously, the environmentalists, and everybody else for that matter, should be screaming at the top of their lungs at their congressmen, senators, corporate and political leaders to commence the largest possible program for the development and deployment of energy alternatives right now. Because, 1. These alternatives cannot be built without fossil fuels. 2. It will take a long time before we can build enough to even make a dent in the fossil fuel use stream, and 3. It is these alternatives, and the alternatives alone that offer us any degree of hope in the future of America and the Island Planet.

"The Howlies would not believe it Ben, who could blame them really, for two hundred years the coal and oil and gas had done the hard work, life had grown richer and more rewarding, almost no one had been required to live off the land for generations. It was like listening to a foreign language, it simply did not make sense, so they ignored the evidence, no one wanted to hear the truth anyway, so their leaders never spoke of it, no one was willing to give up even the most obscene luxuries, so no one did, until it was way too late.

We were fortunate as Chief Oscar saw the wisdom hidden in the Arioi ways, and once he convinced the priests to get their bad habits under control the people started to listen, pretty soon they became our environmentalists, and the people decided some of their endlessly irritating Tapu's started to make sense. So far it's worked, we never ran out of food at least, and the Flox never made it to the islands, and hey, compared to what the Howlie's went through. Well...Life has been kind.

Part Two

Solutions

"In our obsession with antagonisms of the moment, we often forget how much unites all the members of humanity. Perhaps we need some outside, universal threat to make us recognize this common bond."

President Ronald Reagan speaking to the General Assembly of the United Nations on September 21, 1987.

We have met that threat, it is us.

Chapter Five
The Arcadian Protocol

Arcadia is an area of rolling forested hills in the Peloponnesian region of Southern Greece, once ruled by the great God Pan. Thinly inhabited by shepherds and woodsman, it had a nearly ideal climate and was considered to be one of the garden areas of the birthplace of democracy, immortalized in the historical lexicon through the works of the great Roman poet Virgil. In Romance times it came to represent the exemplary idyllic earthly paradise, a place almost beyond time where people could live happily in healthy co-operation with nature essentially forever.

Our ultimate goal should be nothing less than the re-creation of the Earth as a self-sustaining garden planet, capable of carrying the human race and the life it shares through the desert sea of space, hopefully, for the four billion future years allowed by our star. Whether we will reach the fullness of that goal is most likely entirely up to us. It is idealistic, but anything that moves us towards it is unquestionably better than the clearly arriving alternatives that come from doing nothing.

We must first survive the next two hundred years with some form of social continuity. This part is about the generalized regimes philosophies and technologies that might allow survival and lead towards a positive future. Therefore, our first mandate is to define in concise terms the policy set that addresses the issues critical to immediate survival.

1. Recognize that there are too many on the planet and take steps to reduce population in a responsible manner.

2. Recognize we will be using fossil fuels and that the continuing growth in the use of these fuels will result in both economic and climate changes.

3. Recognize that we are the problem and the solution.

4. Employ every possible resource to improve our ability to predict exactly what the results of our fossil fuel use and agricultural activities will be on our evolving climate, until we can achieve a truly objective model of arriving conditions, so that we can anticipate and prepare for those conditions in advance of their arrival.

5. Employ every possible resource to improve our ability to predict exactly what the results of our fossil fuel use will be on our evolving economic conditions so that we can anticipate and prepare in advance of their arrival.

6. Deploy the results of 4 and 5 to the widest possible segment of the world's populations and their governments and social institutions at the soonest possible time in the most effective possible manner.

7. Seek develop and deploy energy alternatives at the greatest possible scales in the shortest possible time, at every possible suitable location across the planet.

8. Recognize that we are one planet and one race, but also recognize the hard truth that mindlessly pursuing economic globalization is a mistake as there are too many people and not enough fuel and energy resources to support them all in an ever escalating condition of increasing demand. Therefore we must commence policies that will anticipate the inevitable effects. These policies must include taking steps

to create discrete regions of economic stability based on alternative energy, agricultural, and manufacturing capabilities that can potentially remain reasonably intact and healthy in the event a global economic, climactic, or energy meltdown does in fact occur.

9. Recognize that mindless globalization, particularly in it's expression of outsourcing jobs, is being conducted primarily for the benefit of a small group of international corporate CEO's to increase their global power and reach, and $100,000,000.00 a year salaries. That in the context of arriving conditions engineering the incremental destruction of regional economic stabilities amounts to economic genocide for the affected populations, and ultimately for the entire planet.

10. Call on the people of the world to make their leaders hear the arriving truth, so that those leaders will be compelled to act in a responsible manner. Not in the best interests of a few special interests and tiny resource rich countries, but in the best interests of the planet and its peoples as a whole, because ultimately those same special interests will find no human race to prey upon if they do not begin to act responsibly.

11. Call on all the people of the world to make a true effort to conduct their individual lives in a manner responsible to their fellows and to themselves, because if they do not, they will most certainly destroy themselves and all the possible positive futures of their kind.

We are *Earthlings;* the abstractions of thought, the words, the grand social and technical accomplishments, the deepest mystical realizations of the spirit, the things we think make us superior in some way, are, in the form and context of *our* experience, the ultimate gifts of *four billion years* of evolving life *on this planet.* The physical structure of our star grants the possibility that we may continue to evolve with life on this planet for an additional four billion years. What we may become, accomplish and realize in that time is beyond our current ability to comprehend. We owe a responsibility to the gift we have already received, and to the future unfolding of life.

We have arrived as a race at the age of majority and responsibility, adults nearly equal in capability to the systems that created us. Intelligence and technology are the reasons we have arrived. Technology evolved out of the human experience because the environment almost always presented a challenge to our comfort and survival. As a result we sought tools with which we could mould our environment towards *our* ideal, without full understanding of that environment, or regard toward the consequences of our actions. Historically the size of our race and its impacts have been small enough to allow the greater system to assimilate our infractions without significant damage, this is no longer true. Our growth and activity over the last hundred years has brought us, and the system of complex life that supports us, to the edge of catastrophic collapse.

Because we are empowered, and because we are the cause, it is incumbent upon us as a race to act responsibly and use the maximum expression of our gifts, intelligence wisdom and technology, to solve the problems we have created. The problems we face now are the greatest we have ever faced, so in order to truly solve them we must find an *inspired* set of solutions. Immediate survival is the greatest inspiration of all, but at this juncture it is not enough. We are adults and as adults we must consider the legacy of our lives and define a greater goal. Wisdom dictates we cannot define our goal's truly ultimate form; so our immediate major goal must reside in providing conditions for the future of our race that will best allow the realization of our ultimate destiny. Therefore our goal currently remains as it has been across the history of our race, to mould our environment with the best tools at our disposal, towards its highest and best realization for our survival and comfort. The difference is that as adults we have come to realize that we must work with and within the environment that created and sustains us, and not as we have in the past, maintain a constant state of war against it. We must find our appropriate place within it or die. To find that place or goal, we must first define it.

The conservation of a long-term steady state living garden planet capable of supporting a significant population of humanity and the life it shares, in reasonable comfort and social continuity for the longest possible time.

If we *cannot* accomplish this, then the entire story of life on this planet, the entire past and future history of mankind, all of it, has truly been and will be an exercise in brilliantly executed futility. It's a conceptually simple goal, but immensely complex in execution and achievement. In order to realize it fully we must first envision it comprehensively. If it is to be achieved we must recognize that current circumstances must be overcome in ways that will yield its secure form, and that to reach the state of relative security will likely require the significant and sometimes extreme effort of mankind, most likely across the next two centuries.

So the first step is to define the goal in the most comprehensive form possible so that we can find the inspiration needed, and so that we can look back from the future's goal now, and find the pathways that best lead to its realization with greater surety than simply trying to blindly solve the immediate problems and hope for the best.

It's only in the last few years that technology has granted us tools that allow us with authority, to comprehensively define our desired future planet, and the responsible pathways across time that lead towards its realization. It seems appropriate to label our brave new vision of a paradise Earth, Arcadia.

The Arcadian Project

To comprehensively define the highest and best long term steady state condition for the Earth and mankind upon the Earth. Then to comprehensively define in sophisticated and responsible terms, using the most powerful tools we have, the pathways that lead towards its realization. Recognizing as we do that the pathways we chose must embrace the goal inclusive solutions to the major problems that face our near future history.

The process of comprehensively defining anything is called modeling. In recent years computational evolution has allowed the process of modeling to reach a remarkable level of sophistication reliability and translation credibility. Perhaps our most sophisticated examples of modeling have arrived fortuitously from the fields of predictive weather and climate modeling. Indeed it is exactly these models in concert with related scientific research that have granted us an understanding of the effects and potential effects of our unrestrained activities on the biosphere of the planet. Unfortunately, to date the full and credible impact of the resulting realizations continues to reside largely within the confines of a small and select group of scientists, often subject to the policies of the government and academic agencies that support them.

It is a fact that a small group of men, no matter how intelligent, cloistered in a small dark room, will not be sufficient to realize and implement the solutions needed to solve the meta class of problems currently facing the race and the planet. The entire race of mankind and its activities have created the problems, and the problems can only be solved through the education direct participation and directed energy of the maximum possible segment of that population. The best existing tool for accomplishing this condition is a focused and coordinated fully participatory program involving a new tool that can be understood as the gestalt brain-mind of the human race commonly known as the World Wide Web.

Enlightenment of the Mind of Mankind

The Arcadian Project will most likely be successful if it pushes the available technology towards the edge of its capabilities. In so doing, it yields a revolutionary new evolution in the potential of the Internet. It can thus result in a kind of technical enlightenment of the vehicle brain and the collective operational capacity of the mind of mankind.

This new capability involves two structural proformas; focusing, by centralizing specific 'thought' processes through mating of large numbers of singular human mind-PC parings or neuronal sets with project specific mainframe processors to create operationally focused meta super computers, after the example pioneered by the SETI program, and, the construction of state of the art Massive Multiplayer Persistent Online Worlds, or MMPOW's. For the Arcadia project these worlds need to include a control representing the Earth as it is now, and a goal world, Arcadia, representing the Earth at its highest and best visualization in the year 2300. Inclusive within both structures we need a time engine capable of accelerating trial pathways applied to the current model through the future towards the goal, and backwards from the goal so that we can better understand what will really work through the principles of reverse engineering.

MMPOW's are sophisticated encompassing virtual worlds in which, 'Players' may have fully found alter egos capable of real-time speech, action, and a host of enhanced physical qualities, while fully interacting with 'avatars' of other people from any point on the planet, in any environment imagined. Participants may exchange real money for virtual currencies, conduct powerful business activities inside and convert funds realized back into real world currencies. They may purchase or create real estate in any location imaginable, build tangible homes and businesses, present products and entertain guests in real time valid interactions. Purchase stocks in virtual exchanges based on virtual or real world businesses, attend real time accredited universities and real time lectures, walk into fully found stores, examine virtual products just as they would in life before purchase, receive products electronically instantly, or via mail in a few days from any location on the planet. Take an instant vacation to tropical paradise; practice a real-time visceral exercise of their religion. Think of any analogy to real world activities, it can now be done in any imaginable fully encompassing cyberspace realm with any other computer enabled person or agency any where in the world.

Most importantly MMPOW's allow participants of serious interest in the Arcadia Project to meet within a fully found encompassing facsimile universe *of the project* from any point on the real planet as tangible and operational alter egos of themselves and discuss verbally in real time, solutions to the problems faced. Then suggest to the mainframe operators, trial solutions to be applied to the time engines, or instigate directly within the MMPOW's actions and activities designed to accomplish the goals. This is because in this case, the MMPOW's are dynamic facsimiles of real and potentially real realities.

The running of accelerated timelines representing actual actions and conditions including following our current paths without taking any constructive reparations, can result in encompassing movies of our potential future histories. Anyone as an active or passive participant can experience these futures from any point of view on the virtual planet, if they own a relatively inexpensive and largely deployed set of hardware and software capabilities.

No other engine set can more accurately and graphically predict the results of our activities to a wider audience, and instill in that audience a real incentive to act responsibly and supportively towards accomplishing the goal. Why? Because it will be widely recognized that this is not a fictional movie or a mindless game world but instead a legitimate representation of the potential future states of mankind's future histories on the planet.

It's a certainty these new meta-sites will arrive because the early versions are already in place, it's a near certainty most will seek to enhance their desirability through creating the most exotic, enticing, professionally subtle environments that can be imagined. It's also a certainty that one environment will remain the most important of all, the Earth outside.

Arcadia in Context

It's a simple matter to paint a dark future scenario similar to 'The Matrix' where the real environment has been destroyed, people live their lives in the exotic virtual realm of their choosing, while their bodies reside in dormitories intravenously fed synthetic food, and if we bury our heads in the electronic sand and do nothing, this scenario may be closer to the truth than anyone is willing to admit. However it's unlikely anyone will argue this scenario is a desirable one, and it's a fact that the virtual worlds cannot thrive if the environment outside fails to survive.

It's likely the installation of virtual world participation across the planet regardless of ultimate form will inherently include a variety of positive environmental effects. Virtual products, virtual business conducted from one location but across the planet, virtual consumption, virtual vacations, virtual homes for entertaining, all these things translate to less consumption of natural resources and less pollution of the environment. An example can be found by looking at the energy costs of commuting to a real world work place, perhaps 45-50% of all business currently conducted in modern economies could be accomplished from discreet locations in fully found virtual offices, and accomplishing the infrastructure needed would be economically and environmentally self-justifying at each stage of the evolution.

Is it necessary for all of this to be doom and gloom end of the world stuff, absolutely not. Humans are goal-oriented and there can be no greater goal than the eventual creation of a garden planet capable of sustaining mankind into the distant future. Is this possible? If responsible policies are adopted pervasively in the very near future and available technologies are deployed at the scales necessary within the possible thirty years we have left, the answer might be yes.

Virtual Arcadia and its Implications

Would you rather do real business in a strip mall in East L.A. or from a green glass castle whose virtual tower lords over the pristine forests of the Pacific Northwest on the slopes of the Cascades? Your meetings held on a climate controlled stone escarpment outside, while your body resides comfortably in a small but elegant real home above your small vineyard in Napa California? Zero chunks of daily life or oil wasted commuting. No need

ISLAND PLANET

for staff of employees to perform the host of mundane tasks that can be handled automatically by your personal E-agent, far less time and money wasted on intrusions by real world government.

True, you still have that production facility in the backyard turning out micro grape crushing machines, but they are manufactured by a robotic staff controlled from your emerald tower, (Not fiction but based on The Japanese watch manufacturing model, where nearly all watches are made by robots in small sheds of small plot rural farmers.) Your home's power needs supplied by the sun on your roof, supplemented by the generator on your hybrid SUV, and the grid powered by the solar farms in Arizona, and the wind farms in the canyons of the Coast Ranges.

This is not a fiction from the Land of Oz, possible maybe two hundred years in the illusory future, but a lifestyle that could be enjoyed in similar ways by an ever-growing segment of the real planet's population in less than five years. It's The Virtual Cascades that are located on the Virtual planet of Arcadia, that resides in the *potentially real* two hundred year future of our planet. But Arcadia then can be lived now, and it can be as morphologically complex, experientially large and nearly as real, as the real planet outside.

What effect will this have on the participant's conduct of their lives in the real world now? The most important effect will be the constant asking of why the real world isn't like Arcadia. The answer will always be, 'because I haven't done enough of the right things to make it that way.'

Perhaps the challenges we face on this planet represent a test intrinsically implanted by the greatest terra-forming technicians of our universe's ancient history, a subtle form of programming buried in the DNA technology. After all is said and done the morphologies of evolution that lead to intelligence are easy enough to predict, and the morphologies of a race of intelligent beings on a discrete location are also easy enough to predict. The histories will always be different but also possess similarities that can be predicted. Foremost of these is the likelihood that intelligence will lead to significant success for the species that finds it, and that success will lead to overpopulation and the inherent threat to the evolutionary system that created it.

The final test resides in whether or not that population will find the most important aspect of intelligence in time to avert its own destruction, and the destruction of the system as a whole. That most important weapon against failure is called wisdom. Perhaps, once that race has proven itself by using wisdom, with intelligence and technology, to achieve long-term positive and

57

constructive existence within and for the terra-forming technology, it's recognized by the greater community as having arrived at the age of majority, and invited to participate as adults in the larger community of creation.

This could be nothing more than fantasy, maybe we are indeed alone, and evolution is an amazing accident. If that is the case we are the single most important realization of the operation of an entirely secular universe across billions of years of existence. So either way, recognizing and surviving the massive problems we have created for ourselves and using wisdom combined with the finest technologies of intelligence, to provide for a long term healthy existence here, so that our future form can find the answer and the truth, has to be the single most important issue facing the race and the planet.

Planting the Seeds of a Better Future

There is a Jorge Luis Borges' story called 'The Sect of the Thirty', about a curious group of men who decided to write an entirely alien encyclopedia, and then began making material things out of the world they had created intellectually. They began subtly placing these things and concepts into the old world, and soon, no one realized exactly when, the old world evolved and became a new entirely changed world that reflected the alien encyclopedia. The Arcadian MMPOW is the alien encyclopedia, and the comprehensive new reality we might seek to create out of the evolution of Reality One as it is on the earth now.

The mission would be to organically grow enterprises and other activities designed to eventually realize the real planet Earth as Arcadia. To literally overlay a new planet-wide nation-state, capable of growing into a new planetary reality, a reality with its own real value money, lands and properties, government, social structure, philosophies, culture, perhaps religion, and media networks. Arcadia might accomplish these goals by using existing and proven business and development pathways in a set of alternative ways.

All historical revolutions have begun with an idealistic ideology held up as an alternative to existing or immanent suffering. Historically the primary tool of revolution has been violence. It's a basic premise of Arcadian thought that we are now adults and possess an inherent personal mandate to act responsibly. Violence, or even non-violent but destructive behavior is simply not a consideration.

The concept is simple, yet powerful. If a comprehensive virtual vehicle can create a comprehensive MMPOW reality with it's own legitimately viable and convertible currency, environmental, economic and political structures, then it follows that ultimately there is no reason why the same thing cannot be accomplished in Reality One, so long as the revolutionary activities do not conflict with the laws of host nations, and so long as the Arcadian Revolution is carried out using entirely legal and peaceful tools and vehicles.

For instance, any citizen of any country may adopt citizenship in Arcadia, without the requirement of giving up their existing citizenship, if Arcadia is incorporated as an international corporation sponsoring worldwide real world game activities. Viable Arcadian currency may be issued based on stock value of the corporation, and while international banks might not initially recognize this currency, Arcadian banks will and can convert funds as a result.

The initial brand identity of this product resides in the desire for any person to identify with the Arcadian Project. We all want to live in a world that is better than the one we are walking into. Arcadia defines the positive goal, and establishes a focused identity that clearly shows the potential for near universal appeal.

There is no inherent law that says the earth and the human condition must be one of continual violence, pollution, destruction for profit, and betrayal. We create such conditions through ignorance, selfishness, and failure to communicate. It follows there is no absolute law that requires we must die here in order to seek an idealized, or utopian life experience on the other side.

However, given conditions in the world today it is necessary to commit the energy needed to recreate the desired life experience in a subtle and intelligent way in order to commence a path that might yield in any pervasive sense, such an advanced and positive product. Thus Arcadia could teach by media and demonstration, while serving as the galvanizing vehicle that directs human energy towards the serious measures that must be taken to insure our survival and then perhaps yield a better world on the other side of time.

It was Hina Day, the quarterly Arioi celebration of the Earth Goddess that took place at the solstices and equinoxes. Arioi chapters all over the islands trucked appropriate numbers of fruit and nut tree seedlings to selected locations, and had folks show up in leis and pareus, every person then filed by the nursery stock and selected their tree to plant, then off they went to do their ceremonial tree planting to the accompaniment of a local drum band. In the early days of the Hina ceremonies, the priests had tried to use Hina as an excuse to get some public sex into the mix, ostensibly as an invocation of fertility. Of course the people were no longer as primitive as they had been in the ancient days and the public fertility rites never really caught on. Nevertheless, in the evenings after the great luaus the rare solitary soul strolling through the late night villages could not help but notice the palpable sense of passion that quietly floated just beyond the edge of the frangipani permeating the night air.

Chapter Six
Terraforming and Social Engineering

One of the most dramatic disciplines of modern science is known as terraforming. The most common example is the study of how to do things to Mars so that eventually it might end up looking more like Earth, partly because in the likely event we manage to destroy the planet we already live on it would be nice to have someplace else to go, and as inhospitable as it is, Mars is virtually the only candidate out there capable of playing this role in the foreseeable future.

It may seem perverse to some academics but perhaps it makes more sense right now to apply the sciences of terraforming and social engineering to the planet we already live on, so that we can find sufficient future to terra-form Mars at our leisure.

In effect, our combined activities over the last century are a type of terraforming exercise. Problem is we currently have no real idea what our goal is beyond immediate survival, or immediate acquisition of money and things, and no real idea exactly what the new earth we are in the process of creating is going to look like. It is certain that any undesired significant change from the near ideal earthly climate and related conditions we have enjoyed for the last ten thousand years will involve human suffering and adaptation, with the very real possibility of human extinction.

On the one hand we are running out of fuel and desperately need to bring every possible resource into play right now to avoid a world wide economic meltdown, but if we do that we dramatically increase the likelihood that the planet and its climate will react against us violently with fire or ice or both, with the possibility that it may eventually decide to destroy all of us.

We must recognize that we need fossil fuels for the time being, but also recognize the damage they and we are causing to our future and ourselves by using them. Therefore the Arcadian approach says use fossil fuels but make an all out effort, government subsidies, educational directives, think tanks, and research support for tools and systems that can serve as quickly and as effectively as possible to clean up the results of using this energy, while at the same time ramping up and applying the same enhanced levels of energy to seeking alternatives that might not be as damaging. Collectively we are the single most powerful terraforming engine on this planet; therefore the pervasive alteration of human activities and conditions becomes the most efficient way to terraform towards an Arcadian goal.

The following represents a potential offering towards defining primary Arcadian philosophies, to be used as social engineering vehicles directed at terraforming the earth.

1. **Reduce the population:** But do it as gently as possible.

2. **Responsible Altruistic Self Interest:** First realize that consumerists and environmentalists are not necessarily enemies and get everyone on the same team. Environmentalists should realize that the society they live in and that has granted a generalized lifestyle of sufficiency that allows them to worry about the general environment, was largely created by consumer economics, while corporate leaders must come to realize that if they do not incorporate real environmental responsibility into their policies and activities there may well be no consumers left to support their institutions, and that this includes their activities overseas as well. We need to finally admit that ultimately all of us, and all of our activities are driven at the most basic level by self-interest, and that in the context of arriving conditions that self-interest is best served by incorporating the philosophies of responsibility and altruism. All of us need to seriously think about what we are doing in the context of the implications and results of what we are doing to the future we are walking into. The human race is now a truly global village living on a tiny island planet, at all levels of interpretation we need to realize at a personal level, that we cannot do it alone, and that everything we do affects everyone before it ultimately returns to affect us.

3. **Economically Self-Justifying:** We earthlings currently live in an economically driven society. To achieve success in this context, any product or enterprise needs to be economically self-justifying. Rebuilding the planet is without question, collectively, the largest single enterprise ever undertaken

by the human race. There is nothing that says the tools needed to accomplish this task must represent burdens, in fact the scales of deployment necessary to accomplish the task demand that success can only be achieved if economic self justification is held up as a primary directive and test of proposed tools, systems, and technologies.

4. Responsible Consideration: Everything we do should be subjected to responsible consideration in the context of how it affects the immediate and overall future condition of Arcadia. It is a healthy thing to imagine the earth as a living coherent creature, in order to make it personal we can place it in a human context, each of us then become a bacterial aspect of the whole creature. Defecate improperly and the host will become infected, go off on your own and build your own little world, taking everything you can and give as little as possible back, This is called cancer. Act without responsibility and you become a virus. But you want a big house and an SUV, its simple, write to your favorite automaker and tell it you want a high mileage hybrid SUV with multiple fuel versatility at least anticipated in the design, and a clean exhaust. Then when they make it, support them by actually buying it. *Think* about it every time you spend energy in your house, act responsibly and you will save money, feel better about yourself, and likely live longer. Write your congressmen tell him you would rather see your tax dollars subsidize massive solar and wind farms than weapons of mass destruction. We as a nation just spent a whole lot of money and energy telling the world that weapons of mass destruction were an evil thing, yet we are the biggest manufacturers sponsors and users of such weapons on the face of the planet. Hypocrisy is not a healthy thing in any context.

5. In order to win the war and build Arcadia we must think outside the box: We are the problem, and except for annihilation, we are the solution. Right now the human mind offers no completely viable or immediate solutions to the problems, but we must find those solutions or die. This means first the powers that be, including especially the universities, government and corporate research facilities must take off the blinders, and both allow and encourage true out of the box thinking and research.

This means sacrificing careers and resources with the courage to follow pathways, which may often turn out to be fruitless, but which might hold keys to unlocking technologies capable of saving the planet and the race. There is evidence that the energy we need is everywhere, locked up in the most basic physics of the natural world, in the basic structure of water and its manipulation, in new ways to utilize sunlight, in conservation and new efficiencies of energy production and use, in technologies capable of re-using and cleaning up the results of our activities. These kinds of research need to be funded and encouraged at the maximum possible levels. We must initiate a new unrestricted Manhattan Project for each of these fields now, in order to win this war.

Then there is this: Nutty or not, there is a lot of evidence UFO's are real. The scientific community recognizes that the odds we are the only intelligent life in the universe are almost zero. UFO evidence is elusive but significant, and there is evidence that agencies of government around the world have a lot of classified knowledge and perhaps even UFO technologies in their possession. The important thing is not alien invasion or social or religious impacts, but the technology. If UFO's exist as they are generally perceived and recorded, their energy source has to be comprised of some technology capable of solving all the worlds problems outlined in this book overnight. If this is true, it is the single most important key element for social well being and survival of the human race that has existed since the beginning of our history.

If it is in the hands of secret government organizations and being held from the public for protection for the fossil fuel industry, or imagined national security, then this is an act of sedition against the best interests of mankind, because this technology, if it exists is without question the difference between survival of the human race and it's possible annihilation.

6. Corporate Co-operation: The primary mandate of corporations is to make a profit. In pursuit of this mandate they must invest in research and development or someone else will come along with a newer better product and their profit will dissolve. Most companies believe that secrecy; absolute protection of products and technologies under development, and selfish refusal to share these assets is the best path to profits. This is not necessarily true. In today's situation new technologies capable of assisting in the survival of the planet are being developed all the time, but many such products get no where, because the owner companies are undercapitalized, squeezed by larger competitors, or rights are bought and buried by competitors. A company in Japan, as an example, has developed the critically important large-scale rechargeable lithium-ion battery. This battery has a long lifetime, is easily recharged and recycled, cheap to manufacture and most important overcomes heat cycle problems plaguing this technology. However, that company licensed it exclusively to a certain carmaker, which has fallen way behind in the hybrid vehicle field, which among other things means the inventor company has lost substantial profits by not licensing this technology to all the automakers, and the rest of the world is suffering as a result. Situations like this can and are in the process of destroying the planet, and as a result ultimately both of these companies. The world community needs to stand up and say a company that develops a new world critical technology should own the rights to that technology but must be willing to license to any qualified manufacturer willing to pay for the license. Excusive rights do not benefit the community; instead they often become dead assets of non-performing companies and frustrate their employment towards a positive future world.

7. Nationalization of Critical and Important Services versus Conversion to Not for Profit Status: Many fields of enterprise are critical for our current and future survival, and many are critical for the economic health of nations. Entirely private control of these critical agencies and enterprises results in efficiencies of operation, but those same efficiencies are often converted to obscenely wasteful and socially irresponsible profits, which serve only a few individuals at the expense of the public welfare. At the other end of the issue government employees are never required to earn the money they spend, and possess an inherent mandate to grow the size of their spending in order to increase their power and salary, therefore direct government control of critical enterprises is inherently inefficient and does not serve the public welfare. The solution is not for profit private agencies and enterprises, which operate under the control of law and careful external scrutiny.

As an example, the entire economy of the United States is currently being crippled by private debt engineered by credit card companies; this is especially burdensome to the lower and middle-income classes. But credit cards have become critical to travel, commerce and especially small business activities.

Much of the public does not realize how the credit card business currently works. Major banks borrow taxpayer-derived funds from the Federal Reserve at 1.75% interest; combine it with private accounts on deposit in their banks for which they are paying 3.5% to yield a basis. Because it is expected that a low percentage of the loans they make will go into default they are allowed under law to almost magically multiply the basis, sometimes ten to sixteen times. They are then allowed to loan out, via credit cards or other means, a huge amount of what is in fact entirely imaginary money, and in the credit card business entirely because of skillful lobbying, they are allowed to commit legalized usury, by charging up to 27% and sometimes even higher direct interest on that imaginary money. Because that money is the result of multiplication of the real basis, which is all our money to begin with, they are actually paying an average of about 2.5% and collecting interest on that basis of 200% or more. The money they get back, as we all know, is not imaginary at all, but is instead a significant chunk of the dollars we productive people have worked our little hinny's off to earn. They are allowed these high interest rates because they have gone before the lawmakers who are supposed to control their activities and argued that they are loaning high risk unsecured debt, and that because of the potential for default they must get this kind of return in order to survive.

However, in the midst of these arguments it is also a fact that the CEO's of the largest of the credit card issuers make salaries in excess of $50,000,000.00 a year off the backs of the struggling little man and the productive small businesses of America. $10,000,000.00 is enough compensation in this world for any man of competence to do any job and to live a very rich life, anything beyond this is just used to buy hundred million dollar yachts, collect toy cars and useless jewelry, to build numerous mansions to be enjoyed occasionally by a couple of spoiled people. In other words it is money squandered and thrown away, and as a result made dead to the constructive purposes of society in general.

In many nations it is or until recently was common practice to nationalize such agencies and businesses ostensibly for the common good. Even great nations like France and Mexico used this tool in the not very distant past. Unfortunately nationalization is a route to the corruption of power and the crippling of societies through the incompetence of government management, and it is unnecessary.

The solution is the support and creation of private highly funded competitive not for profit agencies and enterprises designed to compete directly with the robber barons of capitalist societies. Not For Profit structures inherently posses easily scrutinized and enforced caps on salaries of all employees, and if they do make profits they are usually redirected towards constructive ends or used to reduce the cost of their critical services to the public. A large NFP bank designed to compete directly with the private card issuers is clearly the answer, the interest rate charged on such a card could be as low as 8% and still offer the bank that issued it a healthy margin for security, in part because the number of defaults it would have to deal with would be significantly lower. The existence, or even the threat of the existence of such a card service would immediately lower the usurious rates of the existing banks through natural market driven factors, and the only government action required to accomplish this would be a mandate of law that required the credit card companies to allow the NFP's to lease the use of their monopolistic mercantile credit card network for a reasonable fee.

Can such a concept be applied across the board? Not under the current circumstances, but under evolving circumstances yes. For instance, private interests and the nations they contract with currently own the world's energy resources. Wholesale nationalization, even though it will soon seem to be easily justified, would be a mistake on a world scale now, as a major enforced change of structure would cause disruption of supply and immediate inflationary spirals that could not be corrected in time.

Also one of the most important lessons of the twentieth century is that socialism, despite its altruistic appearances is seldom as socially healthy, as carefully and responsibly managed capitalism Regardless, oil and gas are running out and new energy regimes must be found to replace them. These new energy enterprises, things like huge solar concentrating farms, could be incentivized by government to be NFP agencies if government offered such proposed enterprises easier pathways to funding guarantees, and subsidies to get them started more quickly, which are justified as they are clearly needed for the public welfare.

These NFP's would then be efficiently run and sell their energy at significantly lower rates to the public, and would be controlled against price gouging as the private market's costs inflated, which in turn would serve to restrain the energy based inflationary curve expected to arrive in the near future. NFP's also offer a more equitable spread of income across their employee base, which results again in more positive effects for the economy.

NFP's are also better than the tax relief subsidies currently employed to kick start the wind turbine industry, because, these tax subsidies contain an inherent flaw that results from their temporary status. Wind turbines are inherently expensive to maintain, which means as tax subsidies decrease with the advancing age of the units, many private owners may find it more convenient to simply declare bankruptcy and abandon their unit based enterprises. An NFP on the other hand, is inherently more stable and is designed to serve the public and its employees rather than the private interests of single investors or small investment groups. As a result proper maintenance and continuation of the enterprise is more likely to occur. NFP designation is by far the preferred format for all socially critical enterprises in the Arcadian world.

8. Plant Trees: Trees entrain CO2 from the atmosphere, trap filter and slow rain runoff, stabilize the earth, provide shade, building materials, food, fresh air to breath, cool the climate, attract rain to parched areas, improve the ground water table for our wells, provide shelter for game, enhance the landscape, cover our architectural mistakes, and can even provide mystical enlightenment.

There is practically no other single act we can personally perform that costs less in time money and energy, and yields so much in return, not just for the planter but also for every other creature on the planet. There are six billion people on the planet if each of them planted just one tree a month; that would be 72,000,000,000 trees per year. In ten years we would have counteracted the effects of deforestation in the tropics, and installed an engine capable of making a significant dent in our CO2 loading of the atmosphere. In twenty years we would have created a resource capable of significantly improving the available energy, improved our fresh water problems, reduced the potential for starvation and achieved a host of additional benefits.

On Rapa Nui the natives cut down all their trees and died. If they had been planting trees instead of Moas, when the first white men arrived there would have been thousands of healthy happy natives on the island.

In France in an arid highland area north of Marseilles a man named Edward Bouffier made his life's work planting trees, and by doing so, changed a whole region of the earth from a desert into an Arcadian paradise. By the time he died whole towns had sprung up, full of people living happy lives, rivers and streams had been restored and wildlife abounded. Bouffier's life was immortalized in a short story by Jean Giono. In the story Edward becomes Elzeard, a simple Shepard who selflessly began his life's work planting one hundred acorns a day. Eventually he traded in his sheep for bees, as they were less damaging to the forest, and then diversified his plantings, until at the end of his life in 1947 a great forest stretched across a once barren landscape. The story is true, and in the authors opinion Edward Bouffier should be recognized as one of the greatest examples of our race.

Everywhere on the planet where people have planted forests the results have been similar. As this was written, a relatively unknown women named Wangari Maathai has been announced as the winner of The Nobel Peace Prize for the program she began in Kenya, in which mostly local women have so far planted 30 million trees in an effort to counter that countries deforestation problem. A problem largely sponsored by the shortsighted policies of the government of her country. We need a great leader like her, to simply standup and say to the world, 'Plant trees, plant as many as you can, wherever you can whenever you can.'

Instead of spending Billions on mindless sports activities for our exercise and entertainment we should be out there planting trees and granting the same kind of recognition we give to our sports heroes to people who become recognized as champion tree planters. It's a fun healthy activity, and every tree you plant becomes a personal friend that grants you a deeply satisfying return, often for the rest of your life. If you get nothing else at all out of the energy you spent reading this book, get this, go plant some trees.

One Planet

We are, all of us, one race of beings, one family descended from a single original mother. Diversified yet one. We live on an Island Planet surrounded by the greatest sea in creation, a sea we cannot cross. Like the ancients on Rapa-Nui we build our Moa starring out across the sea, waiting for hope, yet the sea remains silent. Again like the ancients we are insanely cutting down all our trees. It's a vicious gamble based on blind faith, a gamble we are bound to loose.

Our forest is fossil fuel, and when the last tree is harvested, the forest is gone forever. Without the forest, there will be no wood to build our raft, no fuel for our fires, no carts to carry our goods, no fruit hanging in the garden, no shelter from the rain, or even shade from the sun.

Why are we doing this, because like the ancients there are too many of us and because some of us are drunk with power. Those who ignore the lessons of history are bound to relive them. There's no difference between the ancients on Rapa-Nui and the human race, between Easter Island and the Earth, no difference in the path we are following, we know where it leads, it leads to desolation.

If the ancients had not cut down all the trees they might have built a raft and found a way out of their dilemma, over time they might have learned the ways of navigation, built a great catamaran, sailed across the sea and returned with tales of a great land to the East, a land of riches and forests beyond imagining. Instead they held to the path of blind faith in their leaders, because it was easier, because until the very end the sacrifice was smaller.

Curiously, in the end, the Moa were right; a great ship from an alien world of powerful almost magical technology simply arrived unannounced out of the midst of the great sea. But it was far too late, for when it arrived, there were only a few islanders left, broken and starving. The great nation of Rapa-Nui had died a horrendous and sudden death, with the end of the last tree.

Will a grand benevolent spaceship full of Godlike beings with wonderful unknown technologies arrive out of the great sea to save us? The odds are against it, and even if it does, history teaches the odds are much greater it will be seeking to serve it's own needs, and those needs will more likely be served at our expense.

It's up to us to look deep at the example of Rapa-Nui, see the truth staring back at us, put away our axes, and start planting new trees, both literally and figuratively. Far better to learn the arts of navigation and the arts of building ships, and the arts that only a long evolving future can discover. It's likely there are other paradise islands out there; likely there are undiscovered ways to cross the sea. It's a near certainty that it's better to be the discoverer than the discovered.

In fairness to SETI it's worth recalling that the islanders did not have a clue, they never heard a thing, while out there the greater world was bustling with commerce, new technologies, grand philosophies and riches beyond their comprehension. Radio is lousy as a medium for interstellar communications, and it's likely the greater community out among the stars is using something for communication that remains entirely unknown to us primitive islanders.

How many empty worlds are out there waiting for us? It took four billion years for life to create intelligence here, and once it was created only a couple of thousand for intelligence to create the conditions that herald it's own demise. Odds are there are a lot of living worlds yet to grow intelligence and technology, and a lot that have seen it and watched it die. With a new technology recently discovered we've found planets around half the stars we have looked at. It's clear the morphologies of planetary creation are similar across the universe. It means there are other earths, other islands. It means some of them are there waiting for us to discover. Without us the earth will heal itself so even those places ravaged by intelligence long past will be gardens, and where there is intelligence, some of it may be ten billion years old, what we can learn, what we can accomplish is beyond our current ability to comprehend.

But right now is the key moment in our evolution that locks or opens our door to future history. All we have to do to open that door is assume responsibility, take action at all levels of society, and grow up.

The need for a global nationalistic identity and ethic

In 1969 life on earth set foot on another island, the moon, for the first time in four billion years. In cosmic terms that event was about equivalent to the annual swim of the heroes from Rapa Nui to Rapa-iti and back. They brought back an unbroken egg and we brought back some rocks. But we brought back something else, an image of our own island seen from another island. Because of it, we realized in an undeniable way, that we were indeed, a lonely island in the midst of a great sea.

Soon after that event, another discipline of science taught us that we were all born of one mother. Yet since those events our wars racisms and ideological differences, imagined out of falsity have not abated.

The truth is abundantly clear, one planet one race, yet we continue to destroy ourselves, following pathways of tribal dispute that realize nothing but suffering. It's perfectly fine to have different villages, different faiths and ideologies on our island, but we can no longer allow ourselves to be ruled by those imagined differences, we should instead learn to recognize the truth, and learn to live as we actually do, on a single island in a great sea. We need to recognize that our very survival hinges on the full realization of one island one race.

Having realized this we might re-empower a very old agency of village life known as the Council of the Elders. An agency that has and can never have anything to gain from its own actions beyond the prosecution of its founding mandate. It doe's not need an army, a huge bureaucracy, or status as a defacto nation. It's simply a group of our wisest persons whom we can go to with the major issues we face and seek from them their opinions and solutions. How do we nominate the judges of our Council of Elders? Should they be selected from politicians, military men, CEO's of business, lawyers? No. All of these are self-serving. Instead our judges should be selected from the ranks of the wise. How do we find such men? Communities recognize certain individuals of stature and respect, men of wisdom. Wisdom arrives from intelligence tempered across time by experience, contemplation, time alone lost in thought, sometimes personal suffering, sometimes mystical enlightenment. Strangely we possess it as children, loose it as young adults, and only rarely regain it with the fullness of years.

In the old days when differences arose between villages the chiefs seldom resolved them, instead the chiefs appealed to their elder advisors, and the elders of the various villages in the area came together in a Council of Elders. The modern council chambers can be nothing more than a web site with two layers, one for discussion between the elders and one for the posting of issues to be resolved and suggested solutions.

What should an elder receive? Perhaps nothing more than free Internet access, a laptop, and a small contribution from the local economy, supplemented by equally divided contributions realized from the web site.

The single mandated point of view through which these elders should look at the issues is simple, one island one race, the best pathways most likely to yield long-term healthy and constructive survival for the island and the race.

One island one race does not necessarily mean everyone the same; it does not mean one world economy, one government, one religion or ideology. Instead it recognizes the value of diversity, and that the best solutions for a village or nation may be different than the obvious.

We need to replace nationalism with a new world identity that all the peoples of the world can identify with personally. Whether accomplished by the Arcadia Protocol or some other unrelated vehicle is unimportant, what is important is that it somehow be achieved. Pride in nation, pride in race, these are good things but only if tempered by humility and fellowship, and they mean nothing at all if they are used as tools that ultimately become self destructive, exclusionary, bigoted, or antagonistic in nature.

The responsibilities of nation states, longer-term stewardship thinking and appropriate legislation

Ten people are on a boat with no land in sight, the engine broken, the sails blown away; there is one gallon of water left, and during the night one of the ten sneaks over to the water bottle and drinks half of it at once. You hear the gurgling and wake up. What would you do? You would more than likely yell at him to stop, wake up the others, and hold a court. If you were only a little thirsty you would likely declare the offender could not get another drink no matter how thirsty he got, if you were really thirsty you would be likely to throw the offender over the side.

The boat is the earth, the ten people the human race, the water the oil, and the offender is America. Right now the nine are only a little thirsty. Is America entitled to all the world's oil by fiat or divine right, or is it simply because we are the guy with the biggest muscles? We are the guilty party in this scenario and the scenario is not an imaginary tale, it is the essence of the truth. The oil we are using up does not even come from America, it does not belong to us, it belongs to the world, and to the future of the world.

If you think a thousand dollars a winter is a lot to pay to keep your house warm, you're wrong. To a European or a Japanese home owner the figure for a comparable home would be nearer three thousand dollars, and it has been three times as much for years and years and is expected to rise dramatically in the winter of 2004. The net result of this dichotomy is that people in those regions live in much smaller homes, wear sweaters in the winter even in the house, and get by with a whole lot less energy. They are being responsible and conserving the water in that bottle, we are not. Fortunately for us, perhaps in part because we do indeed have the biggest economic and military muscles, and perhaps in part because the other nine people on our boat are a lot kinder than we give them credit for, we have not yet been thrown off the boat, we haven't even had to endure much censure for our crimes.

However, as the water begins to run out, and it becomes clearer that we must be somewhere in the center of the Pacific, the other nine boaters will begin to realize that they might be better off without us on board.

For some time it has been clear that the league of developing nations usually known as the G77 has been seeking world bank funding, world assistance and release of technologies needed to at least try as hard as they can to develop their nations and economies with alternative energy regimes. It has also become clear that America and the powers that be, called as a group the G8 have caved into OPEC fears that such a move if effective might endanger the cash flows of the OPEC nations. Amazingly, most of the OPEC nations are heavily in debt to Euro-American banks, and this combined with the fact that any threat by OPEC to reduce the flow of oil is obviously terrifying, and more subtly terrifying because it carries the threat of default on their huge loans. So as a result in a strange and somewhat unexpected way, OPEC and the other major powers of the planet are in league with each other, holding hands as they madly run a downhill path towards mutual self-destruction. Unfortunately they are carrying the rest of the world precariously on their shoulders as they run, and the implications of this situation on the health and well being of the planet and its future are horrendous indeed.

Developing nations are largely nations that, because they have never enjoyed the economic strength needed to participate in heavily energy subsidized economies, have little incentive other than the incentives imposed by OPEC and the G8 to move into heavily fossil fuel subsidized economies. Most of them have seen the writing on the wall and also recognize that the net advantage to them of a fossil fuel economy is the same as it is to every other energy consuming nation, i.e., economic slavery to the OPEC nations and the G8. So they want to do the right things not simply because they are right but because it is the smarter economic course.

Unfortunately OPEC and the G8 have been for some time frustrating the G77 attempts by refusing loans, technologies, and intellectual expertise. It's the same as saying that guy with the biggest muscles on the boat is entitled to control the water just because he has the biggest muscles, but you just happen to have found a floating solar still in a survival pack in the bottom of the boat. While you are deploying the still the guy with the bottle and the muscles figures out that he will not have as much power if you have control of the still, so he decides to try his hand at fishing and 'accidentally' drags his big hook into your little inflatable still, thoroughly ruining it, and insuring, at least for a little while, that his power on the boat will remain high.

On a world level this is exactly what has been going on, and OPEC and the G8 could not at this moment be happier with the obvious effect heir policies have produced in China and India. It is a fact OPEC and the World Bank now effectively and completely holds 75% of the world's population's hostage.

The problem is that their plan worked, only it worked way too well and suddenly China and India became unexpectedly huge factors in the energy game. It's the same as if our little group of boaters saw another boat of ten people which initially made them really happy, but when the new boat came along side they discovered the folks in the new boat had no water at all and suddenly our last remaining half a gallon of water, is going to get used up really quick.

The point of all this is that if our world managers were acting with even a small amount of responsibility and foresight they might realize that they and the rest of us are missing a huge opportunity that can be realized with a more than willing set of partners. Since the G77 nations already possess a low average per- capita energy use profile, alternative energy sources can be particularly effective, because they can help more people with less energy, and because they can provide a way to avoid the huge jumps in consumption we have just seen in China and India. Further, the G77 nations can enjoy a huge benefit because in the very near future, as the price of energy skyrockets, their energy costs will lower, which when combined with their lower wages means those nations will suddenly become the places of choice for manufacturing, and in many cases for plain old people from the more developed nations to relocate too. When this relocation occurs the immigrant pattern will change and instead of the immigrants all being poor they will instead be bringing the funds they liquidated from the developed world with them, which will then be invested locally further granting growth to the underprivileged economies. Thus the G77 nations could actually position themselves up and into a leadership role among the nations. As the major fossil fuel world economies begin their collapse, the 77 small and underdeveloped nations could become the leading nations of the new Arcadian world. All it takes at this juncture is the deployment and development of the maximum possible alternative energy resources by these nations.

OPEC, the World Bank, and the G8 now have absolutely nothing to loose by supporting this approach. There is no alternative to oil on the horizon, nobody is going to stop using it overnight, and if things keep going the way they are the OPEC nations are likely to become colonies of the New Federated Imperial States of Euromerica.

Right now we can talk about all this stuff with a certain degree of detachment, but in a few short years people are going to begin dying in large numbers everywhere on the planet as a direct result of our leaders misguided energy policies, while everyone everywhere will be feeling the extended effects. The time to act was twenty years ago, now it is too late to avoid huge consequences, but possibly not too late to avoid the total collapse of society, if and only if we begin to act now.

The role of education

Everybody needs too figure out how to use less energy. We need to start pounding this into the heads of our children right across the planet right now. If we can't find ways to use less energy those children now in school will have no future to look forward too. So there should be a new mandatory class of education called Energy 101, where kids are taught the basics of energy conservation, alternative energy generation, and where young people can find an easier path towards majors in these fields. There is absolutely no question; energy production and energy management will be the single largest most important set of occupational regimes in the very near future.

The world is swamped with attorneys, doctors, MBA's and Computer geeks, but if a child wants to specialize in alternative energy, it has to design it's own curriculum, or lift itself up by the bootstraps by knowing somebody already in the business and then getting all its real training by doing it out there in the field.

We need thousands of physicists right now looking at all possible variations for finding alternative energy resources. It is a fact that UFO's are real, it is a fact that the technology they use is mandated to be a technology that most likely can solve our energy problems overnight. Physics are physics. This means our physicists have missed something very important, and very huge in their investigations of how the universe works. Talk to a physicist in a public forum about such subjects and you will immediately be ridiculed, but talk to them privately after a few drinks and they will almost universally agree there is a solution out there waiting to be found. However, none of them can suggest this kind of work for fear of loosing their grants, or their tenure, or worse, there is a very real fear out there that if you do find something out, you risk an unfortunate but fatal accident at the hands of a thoroughly insulated hit man working for big oil or OPEC.

This is the single most important issue facing the human race, to say there is no evidence for essential energy physics while simultaneously stating that figuring out the permutations of string theory, which possesses zero verification and zero actual means of verification until we find a way to collapse the energy of stars so that we can look at these things, is the height of insanity, given the arriving conditions.

UFO's are real, we have pictures, videos, thousands of witnesses, including the Author, it means somebody in the realm of physics has missed something really huge, and everybody is afraid to take a look in there, because of lame brained peer pressure that is utterly misplaced and ultimately criminal.

General Philosophy

Arcadian philosophy is not mindless Environmentalist philosophy, instead it recognizes human desires and needs, and includes all positive technologies that lead towards near term survival with the least amount of human suffering possible, considered in the context of both human and planetary needs for healthy positive and enjoyable habitation on the Earth over time. It's a human philosophy first, but it holds as its foremost recognition that human needs are best served over the long run, by philosophies actions activities and technologies that serve to conserve and enhance the earths environment in a healthy way, simply because for the time being at least there is no place else suitable for people to enjoy the gift of their lives. Therefore, it's not strictly and selfishly human, and not environmentalist to the exclusion of all other considerations, it is about considered and forgive the term, transcendental wisdom, therefore in its completion uniquely Arcadian.

Arcadia is about survival and simultaneously about raising the quality of the human experience at both a direct experiential level, *and* at a deeper level.

If Arcadia catches on and everyone on the planet gets on the bandwagon, or some great and wonderful energy technology arrives to bail us out, then the Arcadian project might be perceived by history as perhaps the greatest humanitarian revolution of all time. It is hoped that such will be the case; that none of the doom and gloom will come to pass, and none of the dire predictions will arrive. But it's also recognized that this idealization is unlikely. The scenarios that lead to a world meltdown are numerous, and they will no doubt arrive with many unexpected aspects at various levels of disintegration. But even if total disintegration occurs and it takes human society two hundred years to pass though the times of Armageddon's and arrives on the other side with any expression of social continuity at all, the Arcadian concepts will be as valid then as they are now, and the new world Arcadia will still be a goal that can be achieved. We just have to take steps now to preserve the technology, so that it will be remembered, and right now we also need to do everything we can to insure that the worst of the scenarios are avoided by applying the best of our abilities. Since energy is the root of our problems it will be addressed first.

'Aue!' Ben yelled as he pulled his finger out of the yam paste that had been reheating along with the salt pork, fried chicken, and fei in the solar cooker. Ben had taken a few days off from his normal duties at the Commune de Faa'a to help a small crew of friends repair a small power source dam that had washed out in the cliffs above Lake Vaihiria; 'Aue!' Tahua Teariitaraiiti, the Arioi sorcerer chuckled in sympathy as he approached up the trail to the little camp in front of the tiny cave in the cliff; "Do you want me to scare away the tupapau? The eels are angry today, maybe too much silt in the lake from the storm, who knows, they chased all the ghosts from the lake and up into the hills, look! There's one!" Teariitaraiiti grinned as he took a swat right at Ben's neck, Ben was sure the crazy mans hand had passed right through his head, and he watched with a grimace as the sorcerer quickly withdrew his now clinched fist then opened and clap-swatted the maybe imaginary? Ben wasn't entirely sure, tupapau into oblivion.

"Ia Ora Na" Teariitaraiiti said, "Looks like I'm just in time for Lunch."

Chapter Seven
Energy and Resource Management

State of the Fossil Fuel Resource

The world currently consumes one point three trillion gallons of oil per year, and is pumping at nearly the maximum possible level, while demand in the developing world is increasing at over 30% per year. That's 30% per year across about half the world's population; it means if the world's population stopped growing today, demand for fossil fuels would double in about seven years. With a projected population growth of an additional five billion people over the next 45 years, and the growth of consumer demand and energy use per capita in the developing world factored in the actual projected combined figure needed is closer to *four trillion gallons* per year. So clearly even if the big fields in Iraq are brought into maximum production, the Alaskan fields tapped, and oil sand production increased to the maximum possible level, it's a certainty that demand will dramatically exceed production and that fossil fuel prices are going to escalate at an ever increasing rate. What does this mean?

For starters, it's likely you've been bracing yourself for three dollar a gallon gasoline, well, it will get there and keep on climbing eventually past ten dollars. That's just the beginning. Oil is a fungible commodity. Fungible means a thing that can be replaced with another thing to serve the same purpose. There is a good and bad point about this quality. On the one hand it means you could run your car on liquefied natural gas, or gasoline or diesel made from coal, or a small variety of other alternatives; there are ways to add more fuel to try to meet the total demand, but in economic terms it means the value of almost all fossil fuel varieties are tied together, so that when oil prices start going up, so does every other kind of fossil fuel. If a company can make liquefied natural gas for two dollars a gallon and sell it as an alternative to oil, which is selling at ten dollars a gallon, will they sell it for two or for ten?

It means the value of the liquefied natural gas will go up across the board to match the value of the gasoline it can replace. Natural gas is now by far the major source of electricity in the U.S., which means the price of electricity will go up, and if current known supplies of natural gas are factored in, it's expected world demand will permanently exceed supply around 2007, that's even if none of the gas is used to replace petrol in cars and trucks. The same applies for heating oil, diesel, coal etc. What does it mean when the price of energy across the board quadruples in a five-year period, to modern societies that can only function with a massive energy subsidy?

All modern agriculture runs on fertilizer made from fossil fuels, all business, all homes, all transport, all of it, everything runs on fossil fuel, so the cost of everything will quadruple, and keep on going, in a condition known as an inflationary spiral. While all these basic necessities of life become critical, luxuries like big million dollar homes will no longer be affordable and the bottom will fall out of the real estate market, just about everyone will default on their credit, and there will be a worldwide economic meltdown. Unlike the last Great Depression, the next depression will yield far more serious consequences. This is because in the Nineteen-Thirties there were less than one third of the people across the entire planet than there are now, and critically, the real electrically powered industrial society had just begun. Most people were still located in rural areas close to enough ground so that they could usually manage to eke out a near subsistence level living, usually supplemented by a menial low paying job.

Barely surviving on a pocket farm without cash, and maybe a few candles, and whatever sticks you can find for heat, may seem inconceivable to the army of government employees and auto union folks currently kicking back a hundred grand a year and living in five hundred thousand dollar homes. But it's a fact that in less than one year from any point in the immediate future 70% of the population of an even very rich country like the U.S. could find themselves unemployed, without electricity, or fuel for their SUV's.

Your five hundred thousand dollar subdivision home with the fifty square foot backyard will not do you much good if and when that happens, and the reality is that you would be the lucky one. People living in apartments in the major cities will be living in a hell, without power, food, running water, or heat. If you want a graphic example of what this is like, rent a copy of 'Dr, Zhivago'. Pay particular attention to the bit about Moscow just after the revolution, and to what the doc and his family did. This time it will be a lot worse.

Since 1999 total energy production has gone up, but not as fast as the population, so the energy available for each person has been going down, at the same time, the ability to purchase energies worldwide has been shifting towards the developing nations, and demand has been increasing dramatically. By 2006 the only nations in the world that will have any oil available to export will be the eleven nations currently belonging to the OPEC Cartel, and possibly Canada. All other nations will have substantially used up all of their internal oil resources by 2008 or 2011 if they had any left to use.

Politicians in America often smugly claim we have no problem because we have enough coal to provide all the electricity we need for two hundred years, and because we have enough natural gas for another two hundred years trapped in Methane Hydrate deposits off the East coast. If the coal gets tapped for conversion to gasoline and diesel, which it will, it will last maybe fifty years at best, and that includes the deposits currently placed under supposedly permanent protection by President Clinton. Even if this capability is developed with a national mandate at the largest possible scales it cannot come close to solving the oil problem. You can also be sure that the transport fuel that comes from the coal deposits will not be cheap, and that the technology required to convert it to oil will not be in place at the scales needed, in time to compensate for the oil shortfall. It's also a fact that there is currently no practical technology, and none in sight, that can harvest the methane hydrates in any practical fashion, so counting on hydrates to solve our energy problems is about as sane as counting on fusion power.

Why is this happening so quickly? It's because of a practice called outsourcing. Wages and costs go up in rich nations, so that production of goods and services becomes expensive. Company directors have a mandate to make a profit regardless of consequences, so in a world economy they move their production to countries where labor is cheaper; they have to because they can't compete with competitor companies based in nations where labor is cheaper unless they do. It's also a fact that the CEO's who run those companies and whose salaries average 300 times more than their employees, are more concerned with maintaining their obscene salaries than they are with maintaining their employees salaries, or the general public welfare.

You the consumer in the rich nation then has a choice, you can buy a pair of shoes made in a union shop in the U.S. or Europe for $200.00 or you can go to a discount store and buy almost exactly the same shoes made in China for $29.95. Trouble is when you do you send your money to China, and because China now has more money and its people are employed, it has more money to buy oil so that it's people can enjoy some of the good things of life as a reward for working hard and cheap. It's also obviously a fact that those one billion people in China making all those cheap shoes need a whole lot of oil to make the shoes with.

Problem is the oil is effectively all gone except in the OPEC nations, and everybody in the world has to have it. If you are in China and you have just graduated from a bicycle to a glorious little motorcycle that gets a hundred miles per gallon, paying ten dollars a gallon is not a big deal, the net result is that the nations who have the oil will sell it at the highest price they can get away with selling it for, and ultimately, either all of the world's product of value that is not oil will fall into the hands of the eleven exporting nations, or, the militarily most powerful nations will have little choice but to declare wars of acquisition against those countries.

Will the winning nations share their oil with the rest of the world under those circumstances? Not likely. This situation will be particularly gruesome as the nations who own that oil will be fanatically inclined to both destroy the production capability of their resources, and the military agencies that have taken over their homes, so total potential world oil production will actually decline significantly faster than anticipated.

There will be very few people complaining about this conduct, as virtually every nation on the planet with large cities will be undergoing massive meltdown conditions of their own. To be certain nothing, nothing in the history of mankind, not the black plaque, the ovens of Hitler's Germany, or the purges of Stalin will even come close to the evil state of affairs the entire planet will find itself living in.

Now ask yourself, is this what you want, maybe it is, maybe it has a sort of distant romantic appeal, well, it won't be distant, and when the reality catches up it's certain that it will have no appeal at all. Fact is there is no ideal retreat and it's a certainty that it will be a better future if we do everything we can now to avoid a meltdown of society in general. Later on we will offer some pathways towards greater lifestyle security in anticipation of the fossil fuel meltdown, but right now we are going to examine the alternative venues for energy conservation and production that we ought to have been installing twenty years ago, but would be well advised to get installed right now.

Conservation

Except for the OPEC nations America is by far the world's greatest abuser of energy resources on a per capita basis and without question the greatest abuser among the world's nations. It is a near certainty that over the next ten years America will reduce it's per capita use of energy by at least one third as a result of rising energy costs. The question of whether this action is forced by circumstance at the last possible opportunity, or occurs as soon as possible as a result of the advent of personal responsibility, may mean the difference between a total collapse of human society across the entire planet, or a smooth transition towards a post fossil fuel world society.

Make no mistake, it is *not* up to the other chump to reduce it's energy use and suffer a little now, it's the responsibility of every single person in the world, and especially the responsibility of every single American. As a generalized guideline it's possible right now for America to voluntarily reduce it's total energy consumption by at least one third, while suffering only minor discomfort or reduction in lifestyle enjoyment. There's no question that doing this is the single most important issue facing Americans today. It's more important than Smoky Bin Laden the idiot terrorist and his crew of fools, more important than outsourcing, and illegal immigration. If we don't do it now it will be done to us by force of economics and it will likely be too late. As a result it should be the focus of a national referendum.

You can start right now, turn up your thermostat in the summer and down in the winter, keeping in mind that if you don't you may not have a business or a home to condition in a few years. Give up that Sunday drive in the country and rent a movie, buy a sail boat instead of a diesel hog, get a new refrigerator with the money you save. Replace your incandescent light bulbs with fluorescents. If you are buying or building a new house, demand passive solar features, thermal mass and as much insulation as possible, demand it. *Do not buy* a big SUV or a bogus luxury car; instead buy a high mileage car. Use the internet and tell the car manufacturers what you want now, it takes those guys at least five years to respond to market factors so they are always behind the curve, you have to do it now. Think about it every time you use energy, and figure out if you can do without or save somehow. Do these things and we might have a future, don't do them and it's a certainty we will not. You people with kids, lay down the law, and teach them energy conservation, you teachers in school make energy 101 a mandatory class, you rock stars and sports hero's use the media, teach by example, make it cool to save, put your kids onto a mission from God. Every gallon of oil and every bit of natural gas you save is a whole dollar less that goes to support Smoky Bin Laden and his crew, do it and save the planet, do it and save yourself money, do it now.

Hybrids

At this moment technology exists that allows all autos and trucks to double their operational mileage without loss of performance, handling or features, it's called fuel-electric hybrid drive, or simply Hybrids. Hybrid technology allows and in some cases intrinsically demands improvement in key factors. If you trade in your gas hog for an equivalent vehicle now that gets twice the mileage, you save a lot of money and you have effectively removed an entire vehicle from the world's inventory. *Again if everyone doubled their mileage rate it would be the same, in the context of petroleum use as removing half the vehicles from the planet.* Oil prices would go down, and we would buy ourselves some much needed time.

This has not happened because the auto manufacturers and the consumers who effectively dictate corporate policies have been criminally negligent, and because key existing technologies have been hoarded and restricted by non-performing parties, such as the Japanese agreement, which gave a prominent Japanese carmaker exclusive use of breakthrough and critical Lithium Ion Battery technology. A technology that the carmaker has so far done pretty much nothing at all with, except to frustrate the advent of fuel saving vehicles across the planet, while they concentrate on a massive line of overpowered toy cars, dictated by a completely irresponsible California based design group.

Regardless, Hybrid electric prototypes exist with acceleration capability twice that of any Internal Combustion Engine (ICE) car in their class, double the mileage, and significantly improved handling. Here is the Author's synopsis on a generic Hybrid SUV that can be built right now, along with salient thoughts.

The Arcadia Hybrid

A new class of second-generation hybrid consumer vehicle, capable of over one hundred miles per gallon, able to run on sunlight, bio-fuel, water extended fuel, petrol based diesel or any mixture of that group, rechargeable from household current, or inversely acting as a standalone, electrical generation station, four-wheel drive capable, with regenerative braking, and forty-mile range on charged batteries alone. This technology is capable of standardization of primary elements across the industry, and applicable to all style and purposing sets. Further, depending on the fuel used, this vehicle qualifies as an ultra-low or zero emissions vehicle under the definitions set forth in the Kyoto Accords.

There are 1.2 Billion cars and trucks on the planet. Normal industry projections indicate that number will increase to 1.8 billion within ten years; the average value per vehicle is $11,500 in adjusted year 2000 American dollars. That is Trillions and Trillions of dollars worth of vehicles on the world's roads. Unfortunately within the next ten years *95% of those vehicles will be obsolete* because of the worldwide fuel shortages and dramatically rising retail fuel prices. The good news is there are Trillions and Trillions of dollars to be made by recycling the old cars, and building and selling high mileage low pollution new ones.

The specifications that comprise the Arcadia concept vehicle meet the demands for that market, in a design genre that allows zero reduction in model type versatility or loss of market appeal. The Arcadia is a revolutionary concept because it also represents a standalone multiple venue ultra clean energy *generation* device, which, as it becomes deployed in significant numbers begins to represent a powerful impact on world wide general electrical requirements, with zero targeted additional capital outlay, and zero added expense to the consumer. .

One of the image and conceptual difficulties is the perception that hybrids are normal internal combustion vehicles to which a hodgepodge of complicated technologies have been added in order to increase mileage a little bit. However, if *one realizes that a hybrid is a fully electric vehicle with it's own on board generation capability,* suddenly the advantages snap into focus. The image of the Hybrid needs to be, the ultimate environmentally friendly security-survival vehicle *and* ultra clean independent electrical generation station that can be owned for less money than an old style car.

Hybrid Specifications
Based on Technology Available Now

1. Body and Platform Materials: Vacuum Molded Foam Core Fiber Reinforced Plastic, lighter and stronger than steel with a host of additional advantages, this type of coach allows cheaper easily adjusted molds, improved safety, less parts, quieter noise factors, and more efficient coach temperature control. FRP materials are slightly more expensive that steel but come down in price as use increases, and weight savings translate to a host of savings in drive train and suspension requirements as well as fuel savings.

2. Two modular platforms: A. Compact. B. Single multi-purposed for SUV's, Mini-Vans, Pickups, and Luxury Sedans etc.

3. Tires: Single step molded fiber reinforced Polyurethane, lightweight, enhanced durability and safety including long-range full puncture ride-ability and multiple color schemes.

4. Wheel Motors: Standardized modular electric drive motors integral with the wheels. These motors significantly reduce engineering complications in routing single motor power to the wheels, allow instant conversion to multiple wheel drive configuration, easy repair, enhanced traction, fuel and regenerative braking efficiencies, and allow efficient control via simple computer based energy routing. Investigations should be carried out on inverse motor configurations, with fixed axel and rotating outer windings fixed to Carbon or Kevlar fiber tire rims, as well as normal fixed drive motors placed internal to the wheel. Regardless of motor configuration, it goes without saying that all motors must possess regenerative breaking.

5. Batteries: Lithium Ion batteries currently in final stage of development at Los Alamos National Laboratories, and in public use in Japan. These batteries show a significant advancement over the alternatives, carry twice the charge in half the weight-volume, a longer higher efficiency recharge life, and should be near half the commercial production retail cost of comparable alternatives. They also show greater recycling advantages. Sufficient capacity for an 80-100 mile range on flat surface, on full charge batteries alone is achievable.

6. Engine and Generator: High efficiency clean burning modified diesel, to high efficiency compact generator: Certain European carmakers have had for a long time, very clean, very reliable, very simple, diesel powered cars that get 90 miles per gallon. This engine technology applied to hybrids can easily yield mileages in excess of a hundred miles per gallon with dramatic improvement in all other product factors. As this is written investigations are indicating the diesel gensets can add up to $3,000 over a gasoline hybrid and are not cost effective. People want hundreds of thousands of these right now, and the fact is that at five dollars a gallon for fuel an extra capital cost of fifteen dollars a month over the life of a vehicle results in significant net real savings.

These engines should possess inexpensive modifications that allow them to burn petrol-diesel, bio-diesel, water extended fuels, and any mixture of this group. The primary requirement to accomplish this goal is a small EPROM chip directing a small resistance heater in the fuel line prior to injection. Bio-diesel has a flash point of 300 degrees Fahrenheit, normal diesel 185, so a small panel in the car would allow the driver to input the type and amount of fuel loaded and the EPROM chip would adjust the fuel temperature accordingly for most efficient burn. Eventually this driver interaction may be replaced by automated UHF communications between the pump and the cars computer. The only other requirement is to replace all rubber fuel lines to overcome chemical decomposition problems. This multi fuel high efficiency drive train will seek an immediately doable goal of over 100 miles per gallon. They can be air cooled with high demand assist from NASA solid-state heat exchanger chips. A similar set of standards apply to gasoline model, with intrinsic design factors that allow simple conversion to LPG and LNG gas fuel systems, and or mixtures with increased ratios of ethanol.

7. Ultra Capacitor: Standard proven feature on existing hybrids, allows instant engine start and enhanced acceleration as required:

8. Photo-voltaics: Each vehicle should be equipped with a maximal set of Solar Cells on the roof, capable of charging the batteries from sunlight alone. New PV technology based on micro silicon spheres is now available in Canada, which is flexible, highly efficient, carries a long service life and is ideal for this purpose. This makes the Arcadian hybrid the high mileage and environmentally friendly winner; it also makes the Arcadian the ultimate off road vehicle. If you are driving across the Sahara, your engine breaks or you run out of fuel, normally you die, but with an Arcadian, you simply wait a few hours, drive a hundred miles, wait and so on, you can get there from anywhere. Suddenly the image of the hybrid transforms from effete environmentalists toy to the ultimate off road vehicle. It also helps make the

Arcadian concept a revolution in clean independent decentralized energy generation.

9. Coach Air Conditioning: NASA solid state heat exchanger chips: These high efficiency, low cost, low electrical drain chips, mated with high efficiency mini fans, can be computer controlled to maintain a maximum internal external heat differential of 48 degrees Fahrenheit, purposed to both heat and cool, and can be placed in convenient locations anywhere in the coach structure. The insulated foam core coach with heat gain reduction membranes on the glass areas significantly reduce temperature demands and make these feasible. Normal air conditioning systems are one of the most complex and heavy options on a car or truck, exchanging them for these chips dramatically reduces costs weight and maintenance factors, while dramatically extending fuel range, and improving environmentally responsible brand image.

10.Instrument Display: Single screen color LCD. Essentially a laptop display, it can be used to display instrumentation, email, computer functions, navigation and television. Simple safety constraints allow extended capabilities only when the vehicle is stationary. However jack-in points around the vehicle allow all capabilities for passengers from a single processor, extensive voice command and cell phone capabilities built in.

11.Glazing: All window areas should be treated with insolation protection coatings: These simple proven coatings reduce infra-red and long wave solar loading by 85% and passively reduce air conditioning loading by up to 40%.

12.Electrical Grid Interface: Each Arcadia should be equipped with a power inverter interface. This allows the batteries to be easily and quickly recharged from any common 110-volt outlet. For short mileage commuters in a variety of circumstances it may be less expensive or less polluting to use only the batteries, and charge them up every night. However, this is a two-way interface, meaning the Arcadian vehicle may become an ultra clean energy generation resource for the home and business, as well as the ultimate electrically empowering off road vehicle. This capability is what really makes the Arcadian concept revolutionary.

It is this interface in concert with the onboard genset and PV rooftop panel, which allows the Arcadia to become a multifaceted energy *resource* at any properly equipped home or business. Once the Arcadia's batteries are charged, if parked in the sun, the vehicle becomes a solar generator, as well as a very clean and efficient alternative electrical generation station, capable of multi-fuel operation.

Each Arcadia contains sufficient electrical generation capacity to provide for most of the basic electrical operations of a normal European home. This is a significant bonus feature that contains several powerful implications. One Arcadia parked outside and plugged into the household grid will send a small but noticeable amount of electricity from its PV cells alone. This will result in a small but noticeable reduction in the consumer's electrical bill. However a parking lot full of Arcadias plugged into a normal small business would provide nearly all that business's electrical needs from PV alone, and an entire nation of Arcadia's plugged into the grid when not in use will constitute a significant reduction in the nations overall fossil-nuclear based electrical generation requirements, while the additional multi-fuel clean burning generator in each vehicle applied in such contexts means, energy blackouts, brown outs, shortages, can be countered, at least for a while, with minimal additional infrastructure cost investment required. Further, each producing unit will be paid for its contribution, and it is very likely that on average the energy produced by the Arcadia will possess lower pollution characteristics than coal or nuclear-fired plants.

You as the buyer can be fully empowered to take your computer based work on the road, watch your favorite late release DVD in the wilds of Borneo, keep your drinks cool, and your supper hot, with a couple of hoses, pressurized hot and cold running water from any resource, all this independence and value from sunlight and batteries supported by a highly efficient multi fuel capable generator set.

Some may argue that for the time being this is a really nice but marginal feature in the U.S. but keep in mind in the rest of the world, especially the developing world, electrical infrastructures are not always in existence and when they are rates are very high, and household electrical systems very low demand. In these places the Arcadian electrical generation capacity becomes an overwhelming asset and as a result, an overwhelming incentive to buy.

Further as energy prices escalate across the board, the value of an Arcadian vehicle as a multi functional energy generator, able to counter blackouts will increase dramatically.

As technology and infrastructure advances it may become desirable to replace the diesel or gasoline gensets with fuel cells, or even ICE water powered gensets, (See water as fuel below) but regardless of source the basic Arcadian concept remains the valid and overwhelmingly positive solution.

Finally, the Arcadian energy generation set is inherently clean. Each Arcadian will reduce by tons, the quantity of pollutants produced by the car it replaces. According to DOE estimates, an Arcadian style car driven 12,000 miles per year will cut carbon dioxide emissions by 6,000 pounds or more over its predecessor. Each Arcadian will be cleaner than general infrastructure coal, cleaner than nuclear, cleaner than natural gas, and, bio fuel enabled, meaning local availability of zero-CO_2 load fuel across the developing and eventually across the developed world. By doubling the average mileage, each Arcadian, in fossil energy use terms, will replace two normal ICE vehicles, in terms of both consumption and pollution. Eventually there will be a hundred million Arcadian vehicles cleanly and efficiently generating localized electricity, mega fortunes will be made, armies of workers employed, the air will be cleaner, people will be happier healthier and more empowered by electricity, the weather more gracious and everyone may enjoy a brighter future, if we are not too late.

90 M.P.G. Diesels

It's a fact that certain European carmakers particularly in Germany and Italy have been making ultra clean simple compact diesel cars that legitimately get over 90 miles per gallon for years and years. *Old technology that yields 90 miles per gallon!* It's almost pollution free, and these cars are far cheaper to buy than a typical American or Japanese car, even in Europe. If you have one of these you can drive *900 miles* on a ten-gallon fill up. Makes you wonder if Americans might have been the victims of some kind of conspiracy, because we can't get these here. Think about it, if you trade in your SUV for one of these, it's the same in terms of fuel use, as taking *8 entire cars* off the road and you and everybody else gets a whole lot richer in the bargain. CO_2 emissions are drastically reduced and everybody gets to live years longer.

Hybrids have their values, but these cars are simple, cheap, require no massive battery sets that must be replaced way before the vehicle wears out, and if they were widely deployed could make a huge impact both on our wallets and on the future of the planet. If this technology incorporates lightweight FRP coaches, some of the Arcadian features, and then offers greater versatility and sophistication in style and purposing you have a vehicle type that can literally save us all.

There are several reasons these cars have not caught on:

1. In America at least, fuel has been cheap, it no longer is and it will only be costing more.

2. They are underpowered and maybe dangerous. What is needed is a super charger or turbo injector system that can be manually turned on or off, and a realization that if people don't buy these cars the end of the fossil fuel world will quickly arrive and the dangers will be far greater. Airbags and other safety features can help solve this false belief.

3. Technical aspects of diesel use particularly micro particulates, make the environmentalists protest and create legislation that defeats the imports. You legislators and environmentalists need to realize that a car that gets 9 times the mileage of one of those huge two seat noisy dirty American diesel pickups that get tricky special exemptions because they are crookedly classed as trucks, is a car that also produces nine times less CO_2 and uses nine times less of our precious fuel. In doing so it dramatically enhances our national security, defeats the terrorists, and does immeasurable good towards the future of our planet and our race. It's also a fact that this technology can be easily adapted to use bio-diesel which means they produce effectively zero CO_2 when using this fuel.

4. Americans still suffer from insecure egos exacerbated by skillful marketing that makes us feel we are failures unless driving a huge luxury car or SUV. The European carmakers have conspired in this effort by putting their high mileage technology in tiny sedans and coaches that look like a third grader's coloring book caricature of a toy car. The idea is that if you drive one of these you will feel like a fool and a failure and others will laugh. As a result you will learn your lesson and spend all of your money on a high profit luxury SUV. The problem with this approach is that the person who drives an ultra high mileage vehicle is actually far more intelligent and informed, and in terms of being manipulated far less of a failure, and far more enlightened than the fool who pays twenty times as much in real terms to get from the same place to the same place. The solution is that we want four coach types to move this technology forward in America. A small four seat sleek and futuristic mini van, a four wheel drive small pickup with a little bit of space behind the seats, six feet of cargo bed and a factory installed camper shell that can be easily removed and reinstalled, with some kind of access from the cab, a two-seat sports car convertible, and something flashy like the German company's remake of the old English favorite micro box car. You carmakers do this now and you will get rich. Please.

Home and Business Conservation

America is powered by natural gas; liquefied natural gas is an ideal alternative to gasoline for powering vehicles, and currently by far the largest available alternative resource to gasoline and diesel. America's electrical grid is just about the most inefficient method of delivering energy imaginable. If you cook your dinner with a gas stove, even though that burner is technically less efficient than an electric burner at point of use, it takes way less than a tenth of a gallon of liquefied natural gas, if you cook with electric that same gas has to be used to make heat to make steam, the steam runs a generator, the resultant electricity has to go out over sometimes really long power lines then it gets turned back into heat inefficiently. At each stage huge amounts of energy are simply thrown away, so the net result is it takes sometimes a whole gallon of liquefied gas to make the same dinner electrically. The same goes for cloths dryers and water heaters, gas can be in real terms ten times more efficient than electricity, and hey, try giving your dryer a break altogether and using a solar powered cloths dryer for a change, (A piece of string outside) your cloths will likely smell better and you can save 50 dollars or more a month, it adds up. Converting to gas doesn't seem 10 times cheaper because most electrical power is historically subsidized in subtle ways by the government and by economies of scale. However, both of these factors will be changing over the near future, and your electrical bill is likely to be going way up.

It's simple; make your goal a reduction in your total energy bills of thirty percent. Take your gas bill and your electric bill add them up then do whatever you need to do to make them come out thirty percent less. If we do this it means in energy survival time, every year we have left becomes sixteen months instead of twelve, and it takes longer for the price of the energy you really need to become so expensive that you simply can't afford it at all. You will help us all buy the time we need to convert to alternative energy resources.

New refrigerators are now commonly available that use the same electricity as a seventy-five watt light bulb. If you can afford it, trade in your old one for one of these, and if you really want to make a dent, buy a solar powered one, these come complete with solar cells, rechargeable batteries, and ice holding bins, and are reasonably easy to install and free to operate once they are paid for, but cost about $2,500.

Also available are 99% efficient very cheap gas and propane wall heaters, and lovely little fake log fireplaces and stoves, that work with or without fans and electricity, require no complex chimneys or venting, and have built in sensors that shut them off when oxygen gets too low or CO_2 or CO gets too high. They are really cheap, $99.00 to $350.00 for a unit that can keep an entire well insulated house reasonably warm. Unfortunately the short sighted lawmakers that run the California State Legislature have made them illegal here, because they think we are incapable of acting responsibly, so instead of making these available and saving us huge amounts of gas and money we are forced to pay ten times as much for a similar unit that requires expensive venting and is only 80% efficient. As a result nobody buys the best solution and millions of dollars and millions upon millions of gallons of liquefied gas are wasted every year for inefficient whole house gas furnaces, electrical heating units, and expensive bad versions of excellent and cheap solutions.

You people who still live in un-insulated or badly insulated homes, get it done, the electric company and the government will most likely help you pay for it, and the savings in energy use will more than compensate over the next few years.

Energy Alternatives
Hydrogen and Fuel Cells

Many of the car companies have invested heavily in R&D for hydrogen ICE (Internal Combustion Engine) and hydrogen fuel cell based cars. These efforts have been conducted despite major hurdles. Fully 95% of all hydrogen produced in the U.S. arrives from a process called Steam Methane Reforming using base fuels entirely from the carbon fossil fuel family at an average 35% to 90% net energy loss. For every gallon of gasoline replaced by hydrogen two or more times the intrinsic energy of coal or natural gas is required. When combined with a net fuel cell maximum operating efficiency of 80% the result is using the same fuels far less efficiently than we are by using them as gasoline-diesel, natural gas, or coal diesel ICE or hybrid vehicles. True the exhaust from hydrogen vehicles is water vapor, but this ignores the pollution from the processing plants, and the fact that Gasoline-Ethanol and even European Diesel ICE technologies are now yielding ultra clean ultra efficiency venues. Auto manufacturers and fossil fuel companies like hydrogen because it is made *from fossil fuels*, hydrogen allows those companies to go on playing the same social and profit games they have been playing for an extra hundred years.

Pervasive deployment of Hydrogen demands literarily Hundreds of Billions for the implementation of requisite infrastructure. Money that could be spent more productively in developing the technology and infrastructure needed for true alternative energy sources. Fuel cells do possess advantages but are unlikely to make a pervasive impact for at least ten years, and when they do are more likely to be the type that use fossil fuels directly and process them internally. It is true that hydrogen can currently be made by using huge amounts of electricity to separate it from water, and that in an ideal world this electricity could be made from wind and solar. It's also true that such a utopian energy world is either two or three hundred years in the future or will never exist. Before we spend Billions on misguided environmentalist pipe dreams we should be spending Billions on venues that can show an impact now.

All Electric Vehicles

All electrics demand expensive long recharging entirely from the grid, using electricity created by nuclear and carbon based fuel stocks: Net efficiency losses due to conversion and transmission factors in comparison to direct carbon fuel use in ICE vehicles range from 80 to 600%. In other words if the electricity comes from a diesel power plant fifty miles away it takes about three gallons of diesel based grid electricity to replace one gallon of diesel in a normal ICE vehicle. For that you get less range, greater inconvenience and higher operating costs, in trade for a superficially clean and very quiet vehicle.

However in certain locations where very small vehicles are appropriate, such vehicles can be equipped with regeneration breaking and photovoltaic solar cell arrays on canopy roofs. Such vehicles can achieve a range of about forty miles when charged and if properly managed can be operated with practically zero fossil fuel requirements at the generator end and practically zero atmospheric CO_2 loading. Hybrids and high M.P.G. Diesels make more sense in big cities, for long distance requirements, and where freeways are a necessity.

Liquefied Gas

LPG LNG and a wide variety of similar products form easily adaptable clean burning alternatives as fuels for gasoline style engines. Fossil gas reserves are being hit heavily for general electrical generation and it is now anticipated that demand for these fuels will exceed supply around 2007, shortly after the same condition hits oil. However, a new breed of bio-mass gasifiers is about to become available, which when combined with a wider availability of LNG enabled vehicles, smaller cheaper new gas liquefaction technologies and new smaller sized membrane based gas filtration technologies show the potential to have a significant impact, both in the near future and after the advent of a post fossil fuel society occurs. The Author has designed one such variation of this combined technology; it's called IBSEC, for Integrated Bio Stream Energy Converter.

Integrated Bio Stream Energy Conversion Facility
IBSEC 1

Potential failure curves exist in a variety of contemporary baseline support structures, including; solid and liquid municipal and agricultural waste streams, atmospheric pollution factors including greenhouse gases, and fossil fuel supplies. At the same time a set of new technologies have arrived, which, if integrated at appropriate sites show the potential to safely eliminate most or all of these waste streams while converting them into a variety of useful, safe, and environmentally positive fuel, energy, fertilizer and chemical resources. In fact, in rural and semi rural areas such systems can process and convert 90% of the diverse waste streams into 90% of the fuel and energy needs of the local society while producing nearly zero pollution or greenhouse gas loading. Crop bio mass gasification conversion is the primary alternative capable of providing significant transport fuel resources that result in a net zero atmospheric CO_2 loading, this is because crops sequester CO_2 as they grow.

Liquid Waste

State of the art sand based and related filtration treatment systems incorporated with existing sewerage plants allow effluent water to be used directly to irrigate crops targeted for bio mass energy production. Allowable BOD levels can be raised, reliance on evaporation ponds can be dramatically reduced and existing systems can process significantly larger loadings. This means animal husbandry wastes can be add processed in existing facilities without installing additional capacity if straw-sawdust mixing is controlled.

Localized Energy Support Bio Mass Cropping

A few hundred acres of arable land near rural and semi rural sewerage treatment plants can be cropped with fast growing fuel orchards using available tree crops such as certain poplar or willow species with ten-year harvest maturity cycles. On the same ground between the trees, annual crops of oil seed plants such as rape, hemp or corn can be planted. Such annual crops produce significant quantities of oil for conversion to Bio-Diesel and significant biomass for conversion to biomass derived LNG, while high sugar starch factors in the stems-leaves can be converted to ethanol. Conversion of these crops to energy and fuel uses completely eliminates the potential for bacterial contamination of the food supplies as a result of irrigation with organic fertilizer charged sewerage treatment outflow water. Numerous installations and plants are now under development and in use across Europe, the largest in Italy is a project that has planted 14,000 acres of willow trees to fuel a 34 megawatt electrical generation plant, which is possibly the least efficient use of this technology, but nevertheless proves its viability.

Bio Mass Gasification Unit

Based on thoroughly proven technology widely in use as an alternative means to fuel transport and agricultural machinery in the mid twentieth century, a FEMA sponsored study recently indicated bio-mass gasifiers are the only feasible alternative for maintaining agricultural and critical transport capability in the event of serious petroleum shortfalls. This paper was primarily concerned with simple gasifiers commonly known as gazogenes that could be adapted to run tractors and trucks directly from wood chips.

However, state of the art large and moderate scale stationary biomass systems can convert almost any biomass stock into valuable natural gas, high-grade dry concentrated NPK-Carbon fertilizers, and a variety of useful chemicals, with near one hundred percent dry weight efficiency, and they can accomplish this with near zero atmospheric pollution. The resultant gas can be used on site for electrical generation, or condensed in liquefaction plants for use in vehicles, distant home and commercial venues.

Historically, conversion of raw natural gas to useable liquefied form was only practical at very large scales; however, new technologies have been developed that dramatically reduce the capital and scale requirements of such processes. In addition biogas typically contains about fifty percent nitrogen gas, which is normally exhausted through electrical turbines causing significant pollution. New applications for old proven technologies can be adapted to clean up this liability and convert it to high-grade fertilizer, while alternative condensing, drying, and conversion processes applied to the gas out stream can yield high-grade gasoline, and a variety of useful chemicals.

Wood gasifiers attached to cars and trucks are not a viable solution except in long term emergency conditions, but liquefied gas vehicles using gas produced from moderately sized stationary facilities is a viable alternative which can be accomplished now.

Combined Approximate Yields Per Day

Electricity: 4 Megawatts
10,000 gal high grade Liquefied Gas
X gal bio diesel
X gal ethanol
60 tons highly concentrated carbon enriched NPKC dry fertilizer
500 gallons gasoline and or a variety of useful chemicals

From
200 tons solid agricultural or select municipal waste
300 used tires or waste coal equivalent
Sewerage effluent disposed safely.
X gallons of waste cooking oil
X tons of waste and primary starch sugar crops targeted for bio-diesel and
    ethanol production

The bio diesel and ethanol figures are arbitrary as they are based on local availability conditions of foundational resources. Because of its nature, and the adjacent oil seed crops The IBSEC plant is an ideal location for these processing venues.

It is estimated that in California's central valley alone there is sufficient feedstock and ideal locations for approximately 60 such net zero atmospheric CO_2 plants, and the potential profit structure is amazing.

Such a plant located at the sewerage facilities of a typical small rural community of between 10 and 30,000 people could consume 90% of the community's waste products from its local and extended area of influence, while providing 90% of it's transport fuel, and 10 to 50% of its electrical needs in a post fossil fuel economy, while producing zero net additional CO_2 loading of the atmosphere. Therefore it seems clear that such plants should be developed and installed now at every feasible location.

Bio Fuels

Bio-fuels are derived directly from grown crops, which absorb CO_2 during growth; the net result of their burning is a near zero increase in atmospheric CO_2 so long as production continues. Bio-fuels burn with less pollution and toxicity, and a major bio-fuel initiative results in positive economic results for agricultural interests worldwide. Bio-fuels will not solve the fuel problem as the river of use is too large and the morphologies of bio-fuel production result in comparatively low yields. It is also a fact that unless IBSEC style plants are installed to reproduce NPKC fertilizers, or people go back to completely organic methods of farming, bio-fuel feedstock's grown specifically for bio fuel production may actually consume more calories of fossil fuels at the agriculture stage than they create as bio-fuels. However, use of Bio-fuels does offer significant advantages and it's critical that vehicles capable of using these alternative fuels, as percentages of normal fuels be made available.

Ethanol

Demand for ethanol will increase dramatically. Automakers are beginning to consider production of 100% ethanol engines for a variety of vehicles, and almost all gasoline now contains15% ethanol. As of 2002 ethanol's gasoline oxygenation competitor MTBE was outlawed in the U.S. Henry Ford intended his cars to run on pure ethanol, but lost this goal to the petrol industry he inadvertently created.

Recent technical advances yield efficient process enhancements slated to be adapted in ethanol production facilities. These include: 1. On site process manufactured enzyme based wide field biomass cellulose digestion into starches prior to saccharification. Allowing use of the bulk of the feed stock biomass, where previously only select starch and sugar feed stock elements could be used. 2. Advanced genetically engineered bacterial yeast replacements, capable of faster reproduction and survival in much higher alcohol concentration environments. 3. Osmotic membrane based fermented liquids filtered transferal. This allows retention of the fermentation agent in the fermentation tank, and allows continuous fermentation, thus decreasing fermentation time constraints by 150% or more.

Currently, most of the viable ethanol facilities in the U.S. are in the 30 million gallon per year class, and require a $60,000,000.00 capitalization. Because of their size, cash flow, and producer-market-logistical factors these plants exist at the edge of profitability and are subject to base product price swings and the whims of legislation. In the Author's opinion, a smaller state of the art modular plant in the 3 million gallon per year range, with a capitalization of $6 to $8,000,000.00 makes more sense. Such a plant would be integrated with appropriately sized vegetable oil mills and bio-diesel processing facilities as described below, or with the IBSEC units described above. This approach lessons market vulnerabilities, solves logistical weaknesses, increases candidate sites, and advantages base product use into a wider variety of end product venues. This approach means expansion can occur as needed and only when justified, and allows greater alignment with current decentralization energy policies.

Bio-Diesel

Bio-Diesel is a diesel equivalent easily produced from vegetable oil. Bio-diesel burns cleaner than petrol-diesel without the undesirable odors and with reduced micro-particulates, and may be run with no adverse effects in any diesel engine, with zero hardware conversion requirements. Pure bio-diesel may degrade normal formula rubber components; mixing 75-85% bio-diesel with 15-25% petrol-diesel or inexpensive re-kitting of the engines solves this problem. Bio-diesel also has a flash point of about 300 degrees as opposed to about 185 degrees Fahrenheit for petrol-diesel, this makes it safer to handle, but causes problems in cold start situations.

Historically in the U.S. most bio-diesel has been made in backyard shops at scales of a few hundred gallons per week. Most of these shops use waste cooking oil collected from nearby restaurants. Research indicates most are sold out of production six months in advance at retail rates usually twice that of normal diesel, to clients seeking an environmentally correct alternative. Germany France and England already have large scale commercial bio-diesel programs in place and there is a major government subsidized drive in Britain to establish a direct agriculture based program, while a U.S. corporation is currently refitting a major vegetable oil mill in Mexico to service over border trucking seeking strict California emissions compliance. Most of the European companies are already producing at a profit and retailing at prices equivalent to petrol-diesel.

The current process of making bio-diesel is simple and standardized, it involves primary filtering and the introduction of inexpensive readily available chemicals that break the large non-volatile carbon bonds, and then bind the glycerin and related products in the oil. A batch is mixed and stirred, piped to settling pans where the glycerin mass is allowed to settle overnight, the complete bio-diesel is then piped off and re-filtered for use.

Alternative high efficiency production venues under investigation include: 1. Centrifugal double walled, large tank based processing, allowing a single continuously operating process. 2. Continuous low temperature catalytic chemical de-polymerization method, similar to the technology used to crack petrol-crude. 3. Selective membrane filter process. Filter membranes can now be produced at selective molecular sieve specifications. Since bio-diesel manufacture is about removing the large non-volatile carbon bond and heavy glycerin molecules, this last technology will likely prove to be the most efficient venue if the chemical bonds can be overcome.

Unfortunately bio diesel comes from oil producing plants, which require a large amount of plant matter to produce a small amount of oil. If all of the arable land in the world were placed into oil crop production the resultant bio-diesel would replace just twenty percent of the worlds current petroleum use stream, but the crop production would use more oil than the total we are already using. However waste cooking oil can be reused, and crops can be farmed from sewer treatment effluent, or fertilized with IBSEC derived NPKC fertilizers.

Integration of Bio-Fuels Production Facilities

The waste product of vegetable oil mill processing is an enhanced candidate for ethanol feed stocks. Thus, it makes sense to incorporate distillation facilities at mill sites. The new precursor digestion systems digest cellulose content for saccharification and allow nearly 100% of the waste product from virtually any oil-producing crop to be re-purposed for distillation. The final waste product is an excellent cattle fodder.

Ethanol production results in significant CO_2 expression during fermentation, but can easily be trapped. Substantial research indicates greenhouse crops grown in CO_2 charged atmospheres enjoy up to 68% enhancement in product yields. Since ethanol plants will be located in agricultural areas, it makes sense to mate greenhouse installations with oil-ethanol plants. And there is another use for CO_2.

Thermal Chemical Conversion

TCC is a relatively simple technology that can take any product with a potentially high oil or fat content, manure solids, coal waste (known as coal culm or lignite), oil seed crops, palm oil plants, ground coconut meat and a variety of other candidate streams and convert it at a rate of about 40-60% of the dry mass weight into a raw oil product which can then be processed using again simple procedures related to bio-diesel processing to yield a diesel analog that can be used to run any diesel engine or turbine with very minor modifications and sometimes none at all.

Essentially you take whatever appropriate material you have on hand, grind it up, add a little water and mix to make a thick slurry, apply heat, about 180 to 300 degrees centigrade, and pressure, and inject Carbon Dioxide, wait about half an hour, then release the mass into a tank and the entire potential oil content of the product quickly floats to the top, the water stays in the middle and the solids like char and ash, dirt, and heavy metals drops to the bottom for easy disposal. You can prove it for yourself by using a simple old-fashioned Presto Pressure cooker on the top of your kitchen stove, but it would take a long time to make enough oil to serve any purpose and it's not recommended as you could mess up your kitchen and stink up the house.

However, simple continuous feed systems based on easily obtainable hardware have been designed that could be located near any significant fuel stock and produce in significant quantity. If the basic fuel stock is free, the operator can make a significant profit and easily pay for the cost of the unit.

As an example The U.S. produces 280 million pigs per year, each of these pigs produces about ten pounds of waste per day; this waste has become a major environmental problem especially in the East where fresh water resources are being destroyed. If all of the pig waste in the U.S. were TCC processed there would be almost no water pollution problem, methane contributions to the atmosphere would be dramatically reduced, and traded for a much smaller CO_2 loading through burning the resultant diesel. Since methane is twenty times stronger as a greenhouse gas the net reduction in impact would be on the order of 2000 percent, and sufficient diesel might be produced to equal a few days worth of the total U.S. consumption of petroleum.

Another example of this technology resides in processing coal waste. The U.S. is very picky about the quality of the coal it uses; this has been true since the very beginning of the industrial revolution. As a result a very large percentage of the coal mined is thrown away, this product is called coal culm, most of this is actually composed of low grade coal called lignite, or has a high sulfur content, which contributes to acid rain if burned in power plants. Lignite also normally has a higher water content than high-grade coal so it makes a lot of steam, which carries particulates into the atmosphere, which makes pollution, acid rain and thick fog.

In modern strip mining, coal culm is commonly reburied as the land is repaired after the high-grade coal is mined; this is a result of shortsighted environmentalist pressures and is a mistake in the context of the arriving fossil fuel shortages. Fortunately, in the old days, coal culm was simply piled up in hills near the old mines where it remains to this day polluting local water resources and generally existing as an esthetic and environmental hazard. Coal culm can be processed using small scale TCC processors and large scale systems that use related technologies, and converted to oil and or diesel at a rate of about four barrels of oil per ton of coal culm.

The TCC and related technologies can be easily adjusted to create a final product which has almost all of the sulfur and other undesirables removed from the oil, so you can easily get a very clean burning diesel substitute.

In one area of Pennsylvania alone it has been estimated that there are over one billion barrels of coal culm oil, lying about on the surface waiting to be harvested, and in 2003 construction of a $380 million dollar plant designed to process this resource began. The end result will be a very large quantity of land recovered that can be used for agriculture, or rural development alternatives.

So this one area could provide 17% of the total U.S consumption of oil during one year. Unfortunately, unlike the pig manure resource once this coal waste is used up, it's all gone.

But because this is a process that can be quickly deployed and if done at an appropriate scales could add significantly to the U.S. fuel demand it will be critical to install a processing base quickly in order to buy time. Careful examination should also be applied to the currently reburied coal waste from active strip mining operations. The process could increase profits to these operations and improve national security.

It may sound yucky, but TCC processing can also be applied to human waste as well. While human yields are not as high per capita as they are per pigita, we do produce a lot of waste, which is expensive to treat and is more often than not a continuing pollution problem. TCC technology applied to treat sewerage treatment plant sludge could turn what is currently a major tax burden and pollution factor in modern societies into a profit-making venue nearly free of pollution problems.

Water Fuel Technologies

In the U.S., Federal loan guarantees, grants, private capital, research for bio-fuels installations and relevant improvements in technology have been somewhat restricted by the existence of a small company in Reno Nevada, based on a few patents developed with altruistic intentions, directed at cleaning the environment and reducing dependence on petrol fuels. This negative bio-fuel condition has been created by independent analytical papers, which ignore the potential that may be realized if or when that company's technologies are applied towards the bio-fuels.

In 1996 the company performed a rollout of its initial product line, a multi-purpose liquid fuel comprised of 50% Naphtha and 50% tap water, emulsified by a set of patented chemicals. It worked in both gasoline and diesel engines with minor modifications, at a retail fuel cost projected to be about half that of respective petrol fuels, passed a strong variety of commercial and federal tests and received important certifications, demonstrated an emissions compliance level well beyond any alternative liquid fuel, a mile per gallon increase of nearly 25%, and a variety of beneficial engine cleaning and running advantages.

By that time the company had demonstrated its fuel-H2O binding technology could be applied to a wide variety of petrol-based fuels with similar advantages. Recent product evolutions include the binding of normal diesel with purified water as a direct, cleaner burning higher efficiency fuel in unmodified diesel engines.

Adding water to gasoline and diesel may sound bogus but it has been done since world war two in aircraft engines primarily to aid in engine cooling, and improve fuel-burning efficiency.

An obscure un-related under-funded researcher has also found an alternative but relatively simple way to treat water so that it will automatically entrain oil and related products, but the researcher has been concentrating on applications in the perfume and pharmaceutical industries. This alternative technology might be applied to fuel streams, as a cheaper more efficient alternative to existing chemical based methods.

Based on evidence already proven by aeronautical engine use and other research it seems clear that by using this new technology, a number of pervasive ICE engine fuels and bio generated fuels may be mixed with at least one third water, to yield a superior cleaner fuel with little or no alteration to existing engines. If deployed across the industry this technology is capable of cutting oil consumption by at least one third, i.e., it could save over three hundred billion gallons of oil worldwide per year.

Water and the Bio Fuels Initiatives

Federally sponsored papers regarding the bio-fuels initiatives point to the potential impact water adding represents on the liquid fuels marketplace, as a caution against capital investment in bio-fuels. The papers indicate the alternative makes bio fuels less competitive. However, this analysis is based on an insufficiency of a few powerful realizations.

1. Water mixtures remain based on *petrol*-water formulations. Given existing projections of pending petrol shortages, if their use became pervasive within the near future, the anticipated petrol price inflation curve might be shortened but not cured. Further, while current water-petrol mixes offer significant reductions in fossil based CO_2 loading; they will not solve the problem. However, water-fuel technologies applied directly to the available and projected bio-fuels streams, represent a true zero or near zero solution, while these technologies applied to bio-fuels now, directly extends their effective value and makes them immediately competitive with existing petrol fuel regimes on a true unsubsidized basis.

2. Essentially all commercially extracted vegetable oils are currently processed using variations of the solvent method. The prevalent solvent used in this process is petroleum based Naphtha. To make bio-diesel in the accepted way high oil bio-mass is milled, saturated with Naphtha and the resultant fluid drained, pressed, or screw processed, the Naphtha must then be distilled off leaving the oil, the oil must then be processed to yield bio-diesel. It seems reasonable to anticipate that there may be a viable way to incorporate the initial pre-distillation oil-naphtha mix directly into the end fuel product line, by adapting membrane based single step filtering. The resultant product would be classed as a near zero CO_2 load product containing significantly improved energy per gallon characteristics, over pure ethanol or pure naphtha mixes, and would most likely meet the demands of the Kyoto Accord, while granting continuing justification for moving the bio-fuels based initiatives forward and would thus qualify for significant federal subsidies worldwide.

3. Ethanol remains an important additive in the water-fuel product group. It serves as antifreeze, and like its role as petroleum oxygenate, also serves to reduce Nitrous and Sulfur emissions. It also reduces flash point levels in some fuel mixes, and thus helps solve cold start problems. Finally it remains to be verified, but seems a reasonable assumption, that an extremely clean gasoline alternative may be created via a 50% ethanol and 50% water, or similar mix.

As a result, water additive processes in conjunction with advanced bio-fuel proformas may be the hidden catalyst that moves the bio-fuel revolution forward, by offering the world a near zero load, bio-water-fuel-alternative capable of significantly mitigating the growing greenhouse gas problem and extending the viability of evolving world economies.

Whether bio based or petrol based it seems clear that water additives in one form or another represents a powerful short and potentially long term partial solution to the liquid fuels shortage and greenhouse gas problems. However, their anticipated impact will remain negligible unless or until the family of current and potential solutions become planet wide pervasive liquid fuel alternatives. Thus vehicle manufacturers need to anticipate the product stream potential, and design for maximal advantaging.

Pyrolysis Fuels

Catalytic Chemical Depolymerization, (CCD) or Pyrolysis, and its applications towards the processing of waste streams and alternative carbon resources is a technology set that has endured a complex and checkered history. However, at this time a hard earned general understanding of the process is beginning to yield safer more efficient and reliable systems, meaning wide field deployment is now underway and will begin to represent a significant fuel source worldwide along a path concurrent with hybrid deployment. Depending on configuration and base fuel stock CCD systems produce a wide variety of energy, fuel, and related products. As the evolution proceeds it is becoming clear that the primary product streams of focus will be gases, heat and heavy fuel oil targeted for onsite electrical generation, and pyro-diesel, which is effectively equivalent to diesel. It is possible that within ten years pyro-diesel derived primarily from waste tires, coal and peat; will represent 10% or more of the total diesel stream.

CCD is closely related to gasification technology detailed above, however CCD usually involves a completely sealed retort and as closely as possible no oxygenation in the heat conversion process. CCD is more versatile than gasifier technologies, meaning it can be adjusted to use a greater variety of feedstock's, and also adjusted to output a greater variety of finished products, however, CCD systems are inherently more complex than gasifiers and TCC systems, more prone to failures, and can be dangerous to operate. So the jury remains out on which technology stream will win the race. CCD, TCC, or gasifiers, most likely a mix of all systems will eventually be installed.

One of the important advantages of CCD is that because it is sealed and more versatile it can convert more dangerous waste substances like plastics and medical waste, and serve as a safe disposal technique for complex dangerous chemicals like PCB's, and even some chemical weapons.

Alternative Chemistry Fuels

One of the issues this office has to deal with in the design of biomass gasifiers is the fact that biomass gas in its raw state is about fifty percent Nitrogen. Most existing bio-mass gasifiers simply route this gas with the nitrogen into turbines or diesel style engines where it is burned to make electricity, and the nitrogen is simply exhausted, which in some cases results in significant nitrous oxide emissions which add to the smog problem. The IBSEC system recovers the nitrogen through a combination of technologies to make ammonia, which is dried to make crystallized fertilizer.

But there are potentially many more uses for Nitrogen as fuel alternatives. Nitro-Methane is a well-known very powerful fuel used to power dragsters and model toys. Hydrazine, a mix of hydrogen and nitrogen is a fuel used to power rocket ships because it contains more usable energy per pound than any other non-nuclear fuel, and theoretical work is underway towards a solid form of this chemical that shows the potential to stabilize and double its intrinsic energy. Obviously there is also nitro-glycerin and a variety of similar nitrogen products used in the manufacture of explosives.

Historically, very little attention has been paid to nitrogen chemistry as a transport fuel alternative because oil was cheap, in most cases more stable, and also in most cases less toxic. Nevertheless, it seems clear that research applied to this chemistry stream may yield a variety of products which could be produced either directly from the atmosphere, or from bio-fuel resources, and which show the potential to add significant value to the overall energy resource. Given the arriving need it seems prudent for government agencies to make a call to chemists and fund research in this field.

There is also an intriguing aspect of Nitrogen, related to its electrical properties, which is that it singularly reacts with lithium at near room temperature, and with almost nothing else. The results are toxic so this reaction is seldom researched. However, it is a fact that Lithium, as a result of huge research efforts has proven to be the best primary material for the best

battery we have so far produced. It seems probable that these properties may
lead to a highly efficient lithium nitrogen fuel cell or battery, which may turn
out to have a variety of powerful applications.

Water

Direct in-engine use of 100% water as a liquid fuel source is the holy grail
of alternative fuel research. At first glance it seems bogus, but the reality is
water is hydrogen and oxygen, the ultimate zero pollution fuels for autos and
rockets. Current electrolytic processing requires a minimum of 2.3 gallons of
water and a very significant amount of electricity to produce a gallon of
compressed hydrogen. However, it has been conclusively demonstrated that
water may be disassociated in an open-end cylinder through application of
electric arcs, i.e. powerful spark plugs, and that a microsecond re-spark will
ignite the resultant gas explosively yielding so far slightly more energy than
is required to achieve the reaction.

The reason for the low yield may be simple, there is not enough oxygen in
water to sustain a hydrogen 'burn' reaction efficiently, which requires a ratio
of four and ideally eight times oxygen to one part hydrogen. Thus, careful
engineering utilizing turbo charger technologies in conjunction with high
yield arcs in the cylinder might accomplish the goal. A successful realization
of such a technology would change virtually everything,

There are also indications, which remain generally unaccepted at this time
that water can be used to create cold fusion energy, and may be separated very
efficiently through a variety of esoteric technologies. It is a fact that the
nuclear transmutation of Hydrogen into heavy hydrogen, called Deuterium,
is the result of the simple disassociation of water and re-burning the hydrogen
and oxygen many times over, which creates heavy water, from which the
Deuterium is extracted. While this process currently consumes very large
amounts of energy, it is a strong indicator that there is more to learn about the
nuclear properties of water and its potential as a major energy resource,
which could potentially result in small scale engines suitable for vehicles and
other energy chores. While these approaches remain questionable, the value
of a major breakthrough is beyond all possible ego based refusals and
scientific community condemnations. It makes sense that all possible support
should be granted to researchers in this field.

Fuel Solutions

As a result of research in these fields it has become clear that diesel fueled or liquefied gas engines are the engines of choice for the near term successful vehicle in most of the world. There is or will be normal diesel, bio-diesel, ethanol and naphtha enhanced bio-diesel, CCD-diesel, TCC diesel and CFT water extended versions of each available or coming on line parallel to the deployment of hybrids and super efficient high mileage diesel cars and trucks. There will also be LNG and BIO derived LNG becoming available at more locations as time goes on, and these fuels will eventually be cheaper than petrol gasoline or diesel.

High efficiency diesel gensets are old technologies easily improved through application of state of the art ultra clean ultra efficient diesel technologies. Further, such systems are ultimately dependable as proven by their universal application in the marine industry and trucking, and the infrastructure for diesel deployment is already in place worldwide. It is somewhat ironic, but old technologies have granted diesel the publicly perceived reputation as the most undesirable environmentally unfriendly fuel, while new technologies demonstrate conclusively it is and will be the immediately available choice of the informed environmentalist in the near future.

Concurrent with diesel gensets it is clear there will be a place for Direct Injection high efficiency gasoline engines in hybrids as well. The only critical modification indicated here is the need to address and incorporate in these engines the ability to directly burn a variety of similar fuel types likely to come online within the lifetimes of each fuel class vehicle. These include high ratio ethanol-gas mixes, and easy LPG-LNG kits.

Major Alternatives for Electrical Generation
Solar

It has been said by some that we have nothing to worry about because we can always convert all of our electrical generation needs to solar and wind, and that there is enough sunshine hitting the state of Arizona each day to provide for all the electrical needs of the U.S. essentially forever. This is true, but if and only if we actually build the solar collectors and the windmills, before the fossil fuel we need to build them with runs out. It's like an old joke, 'at the sandbar at the beach, the bartender hangs out a sign that says 'free beer tomorrow' so you go back the next day and the bartender points to the same sign.

It's possible to provide all of the electrical needs for just about the entire planet, at least in the day time, with a mix of solar, hydro, micro hydro, and wind, with proven technologies already available and already working at a profit. But in order to achieve this idyllic state of affairs we would have to initiate a complex set of engineering projects orders of magnitude beyond any undertaken in human history, and we would have to do it before the fossil fuels run out. Can it be done? Yes. Can it be done and be economically self-justifying, i.e. make a profit? Yes. Why is it not being done now? Because of a lack of foresight and leadership in government, because of collusion between private interests, especially in the fossil fuel industries and government, because of shortsightedness on the part of financial institutions that stand to make more money more quickly by investing in oil futures and then watching them climb, because of criminal negligence on the part of every electricity producer and every electricity consumer.

Large-scale multi megawatt solar collecting concentrating farms have been up and running for years, they have proven they can make a profit even when fossil fuels are cheap. If we start building them now by the time there are enough to make an impact they are guaranteed to be big money makers. Solar concentrating farms are silent, produce zero CO_2, and go in the dry desert places where nobody else wants to be. But they are only going to happen at the scales needed if you tell the politicians that you want them now, and the government offers loan guarantees to the financial institutions.

And there is this, for every megawatt created by solar or wind, huge quantities of natural gas and oil are saved. Compressed natural gas is the only truly viable immediately available alternative fuel, capable of replacing gasoline at the scales necessary to make a dent in the river of use. So next time you go to the pump and use your major credit card to pay for the gasoline, because you can't afford to pay for it this month, or the next or the next, think about it, write your congress person and ask them why this is happening? Tell them to do something positive about it or you will vote for somebody else who will.

Wind

Wind farms are going up all over the place now, but again private interests are frustrating efforts, tax subsidies have been minimized by government playing to fossil fuel buddies, and even some rich wannabe environmentalists don't want them in their state because they think they will interfere with real estate values and their favorite yacht sailing areas. Get it together guys if we don't do it any way we can in the areas that are appropriate there will be no billionaires clubs, and the poor folks from Boston and New York will be pounding on your doors with picks and sledge hammers.

Nuclear

Nuclear power is nasty stuff period, but as we have seen, so is a world without fossil fuels. We have been for some time in the process of slowly letting our first generation nuclear plants die, this is a good thing; those plants were based on useful but faulty technology. Problem is the environmentalists have yelled so loud that nobody will even consider advances in nuclear power.

All across France the government has installed really nifty tiny little pellet fired nuclear plants the size of a typical train boxcar, right next to all those exquisite little country villages. They are practically invisible, provide all of the local electrical needs really cheaply and efficiently, and in twenty years of operation have contributed zero CO_2 to the atmosphere, zero particulate pollution and have enjoyed effectively zero nuclear or even operator accidents. The spent pellets can't be used to make bombs, the units cannot be made to meltdown like Chernobyl or Three Mile Island, and disposal is simple and pollution free if carried out with minimal responsibility.

It's even hard for terrorists to make dirty bombs with the pellets, as they would have to grind them up first, which would happily kill the grinders before they could make the bomb. These little units are really efficient because a simple armored car can carry the fuel pellets around, and because they can be located locally, very little of the electricity generated is lost to long distance transmission lines. In fact it's likely if somebody did an unbiased study they would find the health hazards of all those high-tension power lines were a lot greater than the health hazards from these little reactors. We need these now. They will not solve the problem forever because like fossil fuels uranium is a finite resource, but they can buy us enough time to get the solar farms up and running or find the water solutions or the other 'out there' solutions and keep the social structures intact.

Hydro

Environmentalists almost universally hate damns, but damns make non-polluting, CO2 free electricity, store water for agriculture, industrial and private use, and usually serve to reduce flood damage and enhance the recreational opportunities of the affected areas. We haven't built a major new damn in the U.S in twenty years. Why, because of a couple of big failures, and because of shortsighted environmentalists. Times have changed, we can add to our national inventory and we should do it now.

Damns don't have to be big to make a big difference, a small pool in a small stream with ten or fifteen feet of vertical fall can feed a small generator with a four inch plastic pipe that can make enough electricity for several homes, 24 hours a day pollution free. All across the U.S. and the world, there are literally hundreds of thousands of locations that can be fitted with small or moderately sized damns, that only slow down the stream flows and improve the local water tables, and fish and wildlife populations while producing significant amounts of small scale pollution free, fuel free electricity. We need to start making these now, so that they will be in place providing electricity as the fossil fuels run out.

Geo-thermal

There are locations all over the U.S. and across the planet where not too far under the ground extinct or currently inactive volcanic activity remains close enough to the surface to be harnessed. The technology is thoroughly proven and conceptually simple. You drill a hole, usually fairly deep, sometimes it will fill up with water by itself sometimes you have to pump it in, sometimes you have to drill two holes one to pump the water in, one for the steam to come out. The water is heated by hot rocks, and there is so much heat in some of these rocks that a single well can make huge volumes of steam for a hundred years or more, the steam of course is used to run generators to make electricity, and you can drill a lot of wells in a reasonably small area, all you need is water and hot rocks in the ground and people willing to do it. It is a good guess that there is enough of this potential in the national forest and BLM lands across the western US, to make a very big dent in the energy needs of the western populations. Again, it is criminally negligent that our government has done almost nothing to advantage this resource.

Electrical Energy Policy

To make this all really clear; right now American electrical energy policy is absolutely mind numbingly stupid. We are running out of fossil fuels that are the only fuels that can be used to power our absolutely critical transport systems. We are conducting wars of energy imperialism and preparing for more wars quietly, we are giving away the bulk of our national product to a few often corrupt and radical little nations that for the most part hate us for making them rich. Gas and Coal can be used to make transport fuels but we are squandering them at a truly alarming rate to make electricity as inefficiently as we possibly can, and we are doing all this with the full and complete knowledge that there are legitimate and viable alternatives to making electricity available now. We are doing this because shortsighted environmentalists are screaming mindlessly, because it is the easiest thing to do and because the fossil fuel people, whom we have allowed to control our lives, can make more money more quickly by encouraging ever more use of fossil fuels.

So you folks out there that have the money and the power, you folks who run the oil companies and know this stuff is true, get into the alternative energy business now, it is profitable now, it will improve your public image, people will like you instead of hating you, and you will be working to preserve the social and economic stability of the societies that you must conserve in order to continue to keep on selling your oil, which is only going to get more and more valuable over time, and desperately needs to be conserved for alternative purposes like plastic, fertilizer and so on. Or, keep on doing what you are doing now and all of us; including you will have no world left in which to enjoy our profits and our small-minded attempts at being powerful individuals.

'I'm too damned old for this stuff" Chief Nik'e protested to himself as he sat hanging on with white knuckles at the back of the big Proa, as it flew across the lagoon on a close reach towards Cooks Bay. He mumbled on, "Why do I have to attend all of these damn Arioi ceremonies, surely they could get someone else, or at least let me take the bus." He was headed for the quarterly ka wai kapu a Kane, the Arioi holy water blessing of the fish that occurred right in between all the Hina ceremonies. Yazuli Nik'e enjoyed the Hina days but thought the kapu a Kane's were a bit much and a bit corny. The priests got all dressed up and danced about on the big old breadfruit catamarans sprinkling holy water from the grotto all over the lagoon, while the gathered crowd usually watched from shore with not very much to do. Then when it was all over the chief had to stand up on his now wobbly legs and wave his feathered wand which was the signal to the big tanker trucks, which then pumped fish fry from the hatchery into the lagoon, Chief Nik'e thought it was anticlimactical, and besides nobody had ever really proved the whole fish ranching business really did any good, but he had to admit, the market was still brimming with seafood. " Ahh well, " he thought; 'could be worse ways to earn a living.'

Chapter Eight
Other Arcadian Technologies

Genetic Engineering

Genetic Engineering is potentially one of the most important technologies for the welfare of the race, even if a massive energy miracle arrives and nothing changes. But, in the context of the world we are more likely to inherit, it is potentially one of the single most important technologies we can imagine. Many people seem to have an almost mindless terror of this technology, and the resultant public outcry has dramatically restricted research in this important field, this is good as it keeps people careful.

However, the out criers seldom look at the deeper implications. Right now the refusal to allow responsibly and carefully tested genetic engineering products into crops means we have to continue to use massive amounts of complex oil derived pesticides and fertilizers, and it is likely these practices are more damaging to our general health and well-being than the genetically engineered alternatives, which can maximize the ability of important crops to pull nitrogen and CO_2 out of the atmosphere, increase their output of oil, and protect themselves from insect and mold damage through inclusion of naturally produced but otherwise harmless organic defenses.

It has also been shown that GE can dramatically increase the efficiency of production of the desired product on a given acre of land, improve survivability in drought and high salt conditions, and dramatically improve animal husbandry efficiencies especially in the areas of aquaculture.

Most of us want a life lived in a romantic fantasy Earth where there are only half the people, everybody has everything they want, and everything they want arrives from perfectly pure organically grown produce and crystal clear mountain springs, but in the approaching world this is not going to happen.

As Americans we tend to make assumptions that we are the only people on the planet capable of creating complex technologies responsibly, but it is a fact that many other nations are already working on genetic engineering, and their pressures to succeed and deploy are far stronger than our own. This means in many places around the world genetically engineered crops and animal husbandry will go out into the environment with far less responsible control than they would if developed here. When this happens we both loose control of the environmental effects and loose huge amounts of money that could be earned in America through licensing and improved agricultural production.

Think of what genetic engineering means to a starving world. In China the primary aquifer that supplies irrigation to one third of their wheat crop is almost dried up. A genetically engineered wheat that grew with less water, produced a wheat kernel that was just ten percent larger and that manufactured it's own vitamin D and C would make huge differences in China's ability to feed itself, millions of lives would be saved over the next few years.

Fresh Water

Much of the rest of the world is drinking its water out of its own sewers, when it can find even that. With the arriving world impact of dramatically rising real costs of energy across the board, and almost universally increasing populations, especially in those areas already suffering the most, these basic conditions are only going to get worse.

In America it's a fact that we spend literally millions upon millions of dollars and millions upon millions of gallons of diesel oil and gasoline for transport and bottle manufacturing to purchase water from distant locations in bottles with fancy prestige names. The bottles are filling up landfills at an alarming rate and will not degrade for thousands of years. It is also a fact that despite the fancy and romantic public images, most bottled waters are exactly that, just plain water, and much of it is no cleaner or better for you than the stuff that comes out of your tap. Nevertheless, if you want to be health conscious with your water, just use a filter, you will save a ton of money over time, be just as healthy, and contribute immensely to the health of the planet.

Solving the rest of the world's water problems is a little bit harder, but it seems to make a lot of sense for the United Nations to rethink its priorities and it's mission. Instead of investing huge amounts of money trying to be yet another of the world's policing forces and maintaining yet another army, it seems to make more sense for the U.N to concentrate on addressing the issues that cause the wars in the first place. As populations grow, fresh water will become one of the primary causes of conflicts. Right now we need to use some of our precious oil to manufacture literally millions of simple cheap gravity operated water filtration systems, and get those systems out to the populations that need them.

Marine Technology

Currently millions of barrels of oil a year are simply squandered by the super wealthy, as they operate their super yachts almost exclusively powered by diesel. Even now it can cost $50,000.00 to fill up the gas tank on one of these, which may get one couple and their extensive crew across the Atlantic. This is a criminal waste of resources.

Yachting is about enjoyment, and it is a fact that sail power is an effective and nearly fossil fuel resource free method of powering yachts. Sails are more elegant, fun, and romantic on a yacht, and in many ways on large yachts represent a higher degree of status and prestige. It's also a fact that automated sailing systems are now commonly available that allow pushbutton control of all sailing systems, at all scales of yachting. As the world runs out of oil, even the wealthiest will no longer be able to afford their super power yachts, and the value of these hugely expensive toys will plummet.

It's also likely that if the world continues on it's current path, in the not too distant future, all freight will have to be moved across the planet on either sail or nuclear powered ships. Clearly sail power is the preferred method from the Arcadian point of view. It takes years to develop such ships, and the industry needs to make a careful reassessment of the future of oil supplies and anticipate its future shipping designs accordingly.

In addition to sails new technologies are arriving that show the promise of dramatically reducing hull friction characteristics, on both power and sail driven marine craft. These new developments are widely based on a physical advancement this office calls Induced Hull Cavitation. IHC involves various methods of entraining automatically compressed air films around the surfaces of marine hulls in contact with the water.

IHC is based on the same principle as the suspected to exist Russian Shkval class supercavitation torpedo, but operates at much lower speed to power-input ratios. IHC technologies show dramatic potential for increasing hull speed-power ratios in both surface and fully submerged hulls. Basic IHC involves the introduction of layers of air or bubbles beneath and or around specially shaped hulls. This functions to dramatically reduce friction between the hull and the water. Full scale monohulls have been built demonstrating the efficacy of such systems and Navy funding is underway with a small company in Florida, towards development of a demonstration military craft utilizing an early version of this technology, requiring separate bubble generating engines. Engineering has been done which shows a 120' catamaran engine powered day ferry can be built that will cruise at 40 knots with two 300 HP engines, and two bubble production engines.

Great care must be taken in hull shape design, and a variety of other characteristics of the system as in many cases, IHC technology can actually cause a reduction in marine craft efficiencies of operation. Nevertheless careful engineering has been conducted that proves the remarkable viability of such systems if properly applied. The Authors office has enjoyed significant direct involvement with some of the leading marine designers in this field and developed proprietary systems that show the potential to revolutionize both power and sail marine craft.

This technology is best applied to Catamaran based boats and ships and may allow relatively heavy expedition style yachts and even small to moderate sail powered freight platforms to regularly sail at wind speed, and in some cases substantially beyond.

Trains

Because of America's love affair with the car, we built freeways and roads, and almost exclusively among the developed nations, allowed our rail infrastructure to deteriorate in favor of highway trucking. As this is written America's trucking industry has been in the morning news complaining of imminent bankruptcy as a result of rising diesel prices.

Trains have always been by far the most energy efficient on land means of transporting goods and people from place to place. Because small towns and localized economic security zones will be critical in coming years, it is extremely important that America take a long hard look at restoring and providing new rail infrastructure to rural locations across the country.

It is also critical while we have the remaining oil subsidy to begin a process of replacing high maintenance wood crossties with long lasting concrete alternatives.

While it may sound somewhat bizarre it is also a proven fact that trains can run efficiently with both coal and wood powered steam locomotives. Engineering firms need to take a new long and hard look at this old technology now; because it is a certainty that diesel is running out and will at the least soon be too expensive even for locomotives.

It is possible that locomotives may run efficiently on biogas, or bio derived LNG, but it is also a fact that every ounce of that product will be needed elsewhere. Because of the absolutely critical nature and need for transport, and because it is already proven that trains can run efficiently on multi-fuel steam power, we must take a new look at this technology now. It is also possible to build huge new solar farms, slave these to the trains and run the trains during the day only. This might be an ideal solution, but it will only happen if the necessary infrastructure is installed before the oil crisis becomes too critical. Regardless of ultimate form, it is a certainty that if America is to survive with any reasonable social continuity, it will be trains that save the day and make it possible.

"Urumph" Ben grunted as he pedaled his last uphill pedal and breasted the top of the last hill before the short downhill glide to his home, high in the canyon above the Papeari Valley. He snapped the handbrake on the tricycle, wiped the substantial river of sweat from his brow and sat down on the edge of the little road to take few moments rest and enjoy the superb view of the distant sea, across the deep green valley below. Ben was a direct descendent of the now ancient great Teva chiefs, leaders of the first Polynesian settlers that arrived on Tai'iti from Raiatea. Their first villages had been in the wide valley below, down nearer the sea, but despite the long haul Ben preferred it up here in the heart of the canyon, the air was cooler, and the breeze channeled up the valley always just strong enough to keep the forest around his house 'alive'.

His house was modest but comfortable, now almost two hundred years old, the whole 'neighborhood' had been developed in the midst of the Howlie downfall, and was mostly made from corrugated galvanized steel sheeting that had seen way too many coats of dark green paint in the intervening years. It was like most of it's fellows in the area shaped like an ancient thatch Fare' with steep roof in the center, but surrounded by wide covered decks. It was hung from steel poles on a fairly steep hillside just above the healthy stream that soon became the Papeari River after the major tributaries a half mile below the house. The stream ran the neighborhood genset, which gave the neighborhood enough energy for a few lights, and allowed Ben's family to run the precious big screen CV.

The walls were just lightweight woven thatch folding panels hung between the poles, and the whole house could be opened to the breeze. Most of the homes had extensive local stone rooms retrofitted into the hill beneath and the old imported kitchens had been pulled out of the top floor, in favor of charcoal fired cooking areas facing small terraced patios above the stream. Ben heard Taea's voice sneaking its way through the breeze as she yelled at the kids to stay away from the waterfall just downstream.

By the old Howlie standards his home was a stones throw from work, but, even though the Le Truck buses, now powered by bio gas, still ran the circle island road, it was quite an undertaking to get home, so Ben worked four days in Faa'a and slept there in a local hostel then took three days off to spend with his family at home. But that meant lugging 80 pounds of supplies for the week almost half way around the island and then leg powering them up the bloody hill, he was 54, and the trek was beginning to take it's toll, even though he knew the reward that waited down the last bit of hill was sweet indeed.

And he loved the neighborhood's forest, dominated by the great breadfruits and imported Jacarandas planted when the project was new, now lording over the lower forest of grapefruit and oranges, coral trees, fei and avocados, coffee and tea bushes, hibiscus, the ubiquitous frangipani bushes, and those brilliant bougainvillea draped about the porches, and then there was that loveliest blossom of all, he heard her voice again whispering in the breeze. 'Taea" he thought quietly; "she was still hinaaro puai; Ahh...Life is good." Ben chuckled to himself as he glided the last downhill run towards home.

Part Three

Anticipation

"Be Prepared"
Sir Robert Stephenson Smyth Baden-Powell, founder of
The Boy Scouts

Chapter Nine
Self Sufficiency Regimes and Preparations in anticipation, the return to an Agrarian Lifestyle

Recognition

Some twenty years ago, the Author took a trip to Vermont to look at what seemed to be numerous undervalued real estate opportunities. Huge old estates for half a million dollars and less, four thousand square foot farm homes for a couple hundred thousand. What he found was, for a Californian, an eye opener. The big estate homes had all been abandoned and not heated for some time. Once beautiful hardwood floors had buckled and sometimes risen two feet in the air from the effects of the cold, once elegant stonewalls cracked and crumbling. In the farm homes, families of eight had moved their living and sleeping into the kitchens and dining rooms and closed off the rest of their homes for the winter. Why, because at that time heating bills for even small homes in the northeast were often exceeding $3,000.00 a season.

In 2004 they are going to be going up a lot more, and they will continue to spiral up every year thereafter. In 2005 a lot of people will no longer be able to afford to heat their homes at all, and that number is going to go on rising. In 2006, the number of people who can no longer afford the gasoline they need just to get to work will begin to rise dramatically, and that number will keep on rising. To get to work many will either have to abandon their suburban homes and move to inner city locations or make due with menial local jobs, or none at all.

Many will seek warmer places to live, but Florida the historical choice will see a trend towards more and greater hurricanes and the cost of insuring against them will grow quicker than the heating bills in the Northeast, while the critical cost of cooling a home in Arizona will rise more quickly as well.

Most of these folks will not be able to afford the cost of relocating to the West Coast, and no one can predict exactly when, but it's a fact that both San Francisco and Los Angeles are overdue for truly major earthquakes. Whatever you are planning on doing, now is the time, because if you wait until the obvious future kicks in the assets you thought you would have to do it with will melt into little or nothing.

The arriving effects of fossil fuel depletion will be relentless over the next few years, then around 2009 or 2010 several new major technology alternatives, things like coal conversion, oil shales, and hopefully a few big oil fields particularly in Alaska and Mexico and possibly off the west coast of America will hopefully begin to produce at high capacity, and just possibly somebody will figure out how to harvest the Methane Hydrates. Right now these are all just objects of possible hope, but they represent a window of opportunity. If it arrives, it will likely be our last opportunity for full conversion, and the fossil fuel products will be incredibly valuable, not only to the world then but to all the futures of mankind.

So if we can make it with a significant social continuity through to the end of the decade we might find a small chance to finish the conversion while maintaining some semblance of civilization. This therefore is the hope and the goal. Avoid the wars, make personal preparations, conserve in every way possible. Recognize that certain areas of the planet will collapse and take steps to insulate alternative areas with the best chances of survival. This sounds cruel, but the fact is, if no social and economic continuity survives almost no one will survive, and those areas that remain strong can at least offer a degree of hope and help to those areas that do not.

Finally, do whatever we can to advantage those areas most likely to survive with a minimal impact. Do these things and we might make it through, ignore the evidence staring us in the face and in two hundred years, humanity will be a few tribes of hunter-gatherers, roaming a desolate wilderness and occasionally wondering at the great ruins of a once grand civilization.

Lifestyle Alternatives and Preparations

Unfortunately anyone who does an unbiased objective analysis of the situation is forced to eventually admit that one or more of the nasty future scenarios in the front of the book are more likely to occur than any magical and full set of solutions that will allow us to avoid them. Hopefully it will take a little longer than predicted for these big nastys to arrive, but prudence dictates we take a look at what we can do to help get some of us through to the other side of the various ends of the world.

Historically America has enjoyed a sense of security behind the fortress of oceans that insulated it from most of the world's wars and actual invasion continues to be unlikely. But the new wars of the have-nots will affect everyone on the planet. It doesn't matter where they are from or who they are, a person without food, fuel or water will take the basics of life by force if necessary, in its quest for survival. The best defense against such attacks is a secure well stocked home in the country or a rural small town or village; located in areas proven capable of long term localized food and resource production, and within or near a community of like minded individuals able to assist in local defense against the possibility of gangs moving out from the cities.

While this may sound radical, it's a fact that survival supply sales continue to be strong, and will only grow stronger as things begin to deteriorate, and unless there is a very big miracle things will deteriorate over the next ten or twenty years. The act of buying and putting into storage survival supplies continues as a response to our historical fear of nuclear wars and the programming instilled in us by our government that if such a thing occurred you only had to survive in your basement for a couple of weeks and then the world would be fine once again. This was a lie then and it is even more of a lie now. Survival supplies remain a good thing, but, when the fossil fuel collapse begins to occur, things won't get better in two weeks, in fact, the fossil fuel infrastructure and social order we have created will never return, ever. As a result the continuation of social continuity and a reasonable way of life will demand a fundamental restructuring of the ways we live our lives. Foremost among these restructurings will be the need to establish long-term localized conditions of self-sufficiency.

However, if we start now, there is nothing that says this has to represent an immediate and overwhelming burden on our lives, in fact it can be an opportunity to explore an alternative happier healthier lifestyle, and there is nothing that says a life lived in the country has to be one of poverty and drudgery, if you simply use foresight and apply careful planning, you may find yourself happily surprised.

It's become apparent in the last few years that the world's stock markets, whose remarkable performances throughout the 80's and 90's had dramatically devalued the previously almost guaranteed appreciation of real estate, is now in the process of reversing itself, and that at the very least there is a widely placed contingent of the investment enabled seeking alternative and more secure venues for investment. The need and value of business real estate is slowing down as the market grows saturated and people nervous about the costs of commuting and working in high rises and cities seek alternative places to work, while the internet has empowered many jobs that can be done from diverse locations.

All these factors indicate trends will witness a general enhancement of the values of owning and or living in a home in the country or rural small town. These markets can benefit if the pitfalls inherent in buying, maintaining and insuring the security of a country home can be overcome. Further the desirability of owning a country home can be dramatically enhanced if that home serves to provide value as a more secure location for retreat in times of social duress, as a potential income venue, and or as an ideal place for the buyer to dream of and actually enjoy spending its retirement years. If that home allows the owner to participate in cooperatively owned farms, vineyards, wineries, restaurants, ocean fisheries, and a host of other relational enterprises with little or no risk, then ownership of such a home becomes remarkably desirable.

Historically the anticipation and actuality of owning a second home has suffered from certain hazards; geomorphology issues like fire, snow, earthquake and landslide; depreciation enhanced by shoddy craftsmanship and cheap construction. The all too common unethical real estate agents and developers, security hazards like burglary and break-ins, potential problems from wells and badly maintained roads, and the ubiquitous country neighbors with their piles of junk are just a few of the issues that must be addressed to satisfy today's more sophisticated and demanding country property buyer.

In most cases a second or primary country home needs to be within a reasonable distance from the purchaser's primary residence, within a short distance from a small town that can provide support amenities, and it helps add value if it is within a reasonable distance from an attractive feature such as a national park, river, lake etc. The venues detailed here seek to address all of these issues in a way that ultimately results in a comprehensive evolution of the country home into a new type of commodity. A product that addresses all the issues and needs that will likely unfold in the foreseeable future, while providing a multifaceted and ultimately secure value for it's purchaser now, and a significant new and unique set of profit venues, beyond those currently available to the typical country developer or purchaser. It also examines ways to reorganize existing neighborhoods and small communities towards greater venues of economic and physical security.

If you the buyer goes out and looks for a place that fits all the criteria that follows in this section you probably won't find it. This is because country real estate development is a sometimes-risky process often undertaken by under financed speculators, and many of the alternative parcels you will find are the result of lot splits performed with little or no improvements or foresight. If you do find a large project with amenities, usually it will be a golf course with home site private parcels not much bigger than the one you had at your suburban tract home. Golf course projects can be converted when or if the time comes to more productive uses, and if you decide to go it on your own, then look for a private parcel that at least shows the potential to incorporate as many of the features detailed here as possible.

The purpose of this section is also partly to help country developers realize there is an alternative market out there now that will likely be growing dramatically over the next few years, and that if they incorporate many of the features indicated here they will likely find greater success in their endeavors.

In America especially, we have come to be a non-tribe of single family units, where just about everybody believes their neighbor is out to screw them, partly because the society we have built encourages us to do whatever we can to screw them first. So we put six locks on the front door, install electronic security systems, lock the world out and hope for the best.

However, in the likely arriving transition times and in the hopefully recovering post fossil fuel world, localized self-sufficiency will be a key factor in social continuity and survival.

True self-sufficiency is almost impossible to achieve by a single-family unit working alone. That's exactly the reason why almost all societies that existed before the advent of cheap energy, that were not based on slavery or exploitation, organized themselves into extended families usually called tribes. Strictly commutarian tribal life is likely too radical a step for most Americans, but small or moderately sized co-operative communities are not. This is especially true in the rural and semi rural areas, which will be the only places any sane person wants to be as the fossil fuel shortage global disintegration begins.

Self sufficiency is a lot of work, and without the fossil fuel energy subsidy we take for granted, much of the infrastructure we have built to avoid this work will fail and be replaced by personal time spent producing our own food, energy, and other basic needs. Again small co-operating communities are the key to success.

Finally self-defense may become critical. If a gang of hungry armed folks arrives at your doorstep looking to take what you have, it makes little difference how many guns you own, if you are alone odds are they will take what they want and you and your family will no longer have need of your goods because you will be dead. But a co-operative community is much harder for most hard pressed traveling gangs to successfully attack, so your odds for success are once again improved.

For the time being these are all considerations we need to keep in the back of our minds, and it seems prudent to anticipate such a world at this time. However, few of us want to make the end of the world our driving purpose in life, so the best we can do is create social and physical conditions that anticipate such things, and if we can also include in that anticipation alternative lifestyle regimes and structures that offer the potential for an improved healthier and happier lifestyle, and an improved and happier countryside right now. Well, how can it hurt?

The following two examples of possibly successful co-operative country development structures are offered as guidelines only, there are a lot of evolutions and variations that can be made to work, and ways we will address of re-organizing existing neighborhoods and areas towards greater success

Location

Drive Too
1. At least 1 hour from, but no more than 6 hours drive from the suburban boundaries of a primary urban-suburban area, or international airport.
2. Within 12 miles of a small to medium country town, preferably with hospital or medical facility, grocery, hardware etc.
3. Whenever possible the actual access to the project or parcel should be from a well maintained but quiet country road, and not directly from a major highway. The local access roads should be gated but capable of quick access by external emergency personnel such as fire fighters, police, and ambulance drivers. It's important that the existence and access of such projects or parcels be unobtrusive. Such an approach dramatically reduces the number of undesirables seeking access, while enhancing the security, prestige, and exclusivity.
4. In some areas near-ocean properties will be suitable or desirable. These should possess elevation or secure location sufficient to warrant security from the sea in times of storm or Tsunami. While at first glance near ocean front properties may seem insecure, such areas are usually very productive native food resources.

Remote
1. Near entirely self-sufficient communities at remote locations. It is the remoteness itself, combined with the sustainable self-sufficiency, which enhances the appeal and the resources available for comfortable survival in times of duress. Such projects should be located in areas of exceptional natural resources, and include direct access to fresh water. The alternative is to look for the lowest possible population density rural areas of small to moderately sized old farms. People survived and in many cases had good lives in such places before the economic evolutions of fossil fuel society drove them to the cities. As the fossil fuel structure collapses they will once again become desirable locations to live.
2. Proximity to National Parks, forests, rivers or other recreational features, including remote oceanfront. Parcels that border public lands are especially desirable. This factor is important not simply for its good times recreational attraction but also because public wild lands represent an

important resource for food, heating and other basic resources important in times of duress.

3. Geomorphology Hazards: Try to avoid areas of known earthquake, volcanic, flood, or major storm effects.

Densities

Drive Too

1. 1-3 acres private land minimum for individual home sites. Anything less destroys the desirable characteristics of a country home and redefines the development as a negative impact cluster or condominium style project, or simply recreates the urban-suburban conditions the purchaser is trying to escape. While densities larger than this tend to prohibit, (except in projects directed towards proven high purchase price markets.) paved roads, centralized water systems and infrastructure, and dramatically limits the dollar amount of amenities the developer can afford to incorporate in the project.

2. Overall density of five or more acres per home site, or location next to or near national forest or public lands, or community owned viable farmlands. Significant lands or water areas should be available for commons, greenbelts, recreational, or agricultural uses. In states such as California where common areas are difficult to perform due to State regulation, such areas can be achieved through creative use of easements, or separate corporate ownership with shares owned by home site purchasers, or other alternative means. Private ownership sites tend to get developed haphazardly, while common areas serve to maintain preserve and enhance the desirable rural atmosphere, and offer the potential or immediate opportunity for relational commercial enterprises. They also provide cover and feed for wildlife important during times of social duress.

Ultra Remote

In remote locations higher densities are sometimes desirable.

1. In most cases these types of projects must be capable of being as self-sufficient as possible. Infrastructure costs, and thus ultimate sales costs, under these conditions dramatically escalate as density of improvements lowers.

2. Where based on resort community or hospitality venues, homes may be less frequented by their owners and more frequented by paying guests, at least until the collapse. In such cases, housekeeping and logistics will be more efficient at higher densities.

3. Access to these locations will often be by common carriers. This means internal transportation will be by foot or resort vehicles. In such cases higher densities are obviously desirable.

4. In remote locations, a sense of community enhances the feeling of security, important in the case of potential attack by vagabonds, and in a real sense nature remains a kind of enemy.

The philosophy is to seek or employ clustering of individual homes or bungalows in park-like settings, while areas of common ownership are dramatically increased and the importance of adjacency to public lands becomes significantly higher. In such cases density becomes a matter of judgment based on particular site conditions, but as a general rule a one-quarter acre minimum private home site in a five-acre per home site overall density is a good guideline. If this is difficult to visualize think of a small Vermont village transported to the Pacific Northwest wilderness and done in log cabin style along both sides of a forested river, or an old English country village; community at the front door and wilderness at the back, with the living areas oriented towards the wilderness.

Small Rural Towns

Obviously the above and much of below addresses rural residential developments, and a home in a small rural town will not meet some of these desirable traits. Nevertheless, a home on a quiet tree lined street in a small rural town, with a good sized back yard, a good community water supply, and a rural energy co-op based on a hydro facility, will without question be one of the best places to be.

Of course such places already exist, so nobody has to suggest to anybody how they need to be built, and the good news is that because of the modern fossil fuel society we have built, that encourages everybody to live in the city, many of these places continue to represent undervalued investment alternatives given the futures we have discussed. They also represent excellent retirement alternatives, which can be bought now, and rented out until the time comes.

Specifications and Philosophy
Preferred Land Characteristics

1. Water Feature, stream, lake or pond development potential. Such features add to the attractive value of the project or parcel, and represent an important resource in times of duress.

2. Proven on-site ground water resource, critical for community water systems and single parcels. Well or spring water is important because it lends itself to infrastructure systems and because it is less subject to pollution, chemical-biological weapons and changing weather patterns. Never buy a home or site in the country without first making absolutely sure it has good fresh water.

3. Irregular and sloping topography but not too steep. This type of ground lends itself to greater variation, interesting features and privacy for individual home sites. It also allows in most cases for varied view and water-oriented sites, and enhances the ability to create individual parcels that seem larger than they actually are. Some inordinately steep land may be okay in larger projects but should be buffered from home sites by greenbelt and other protective easements. Areas of flat or gently sloping productive or potentially productive agricultural or wetlands areas are desirable. When such areas are available, as a general rule, they should be set aside as managed or potentially managed productive or income purposed land uses and not used for residential purposes.

As mentioned many have sought to establish higher-security self-sufficiency conditions on their own. However, it's a fact that most infrastructure equivalency self-sufficiency systems performed on an individual owner basis, are for the most part inherently inefficient, costly, and difficult to maintain, but when performed on a cooperative basis for communities of twenty or more homes, such systems begin to realize significant improvement in their design, quality, maintenance, survivability and cost per end unit. For instance, a single reliable wind turbine sized for a single home can cost $23,000 while a single large wind turbine sized to use existing lines for ten homes can actually cost much less, often in the area of $12,000. This is because the market for large commercial turbines is much larger than for single residential applications. Single large diesel generators also see dramatic reductions in cost per end unit both at purchase and during operation. Single generation stations allow for quieter overall impact, centralization of fuel storage, better maintenance, and greater efficiencies especially when considered in the context of their most important country task; the pumping of water. Likewise, centralized water systems allow significant per unit savings and efficiencies over individual systems, including the allowance for large water storage installations, and the enhancement of fire frightening resources.

Existing small towns and communities will usually have most of these important infrastructures in place. But examine them carefully, a small town completely reliant on the public grid whose nearest generator is a gas fired plant three hundred miles away will only be slightly better off than your existing location in the city. The best situation in this regard is a local electric co-op based on a reasonably local hydroelectric system, which may be cut off from the grid to service local owners if-when the time comes. The following are general examples designed to demonstrate the logic for the cooperative approach of country development, or desirable features to look for in existing prospects.

Desirable Infrastructure Project Development Features

1. Centralized, secure, water pumping, storage, and treatment, sited with centralized on site conventional electrical generation. It is highly preferred that the water storage area(s) be located whenever possible on the high point(s) of the project. This allows short periods of pumping to fill water storage that can then be accessed by all homes over longer periods through gravity operation alone. Such a system requires mains, but on these scales modern plastic pipes can be used at reasonable developer expense during road construction. This approach also allows for localized inexpensive placement of numerous hydrant stations for fire fighters. In small towns look for water tank towers serving the same purpose

2. Wherever possible candidate properties should be assessed for small and micro hydro electrical development potential. Such systems and support technologies are becoming increasingly popular and available across the world, and if properly installed allow for essentially endless operation and

endless "free" electricity. Such systems do not require large lakes or fast moving streams, but instead may be created from head resources such as very small ponds in streams at high elevations, with water diverted through inexpensive plastic pipe to localized turbine installations. Localized external energy co-ops or the potential for such in the general area, especially those based on existing hydroelectric facilities are also major plusses to look for, if there is no hydro in the area investigate the power source closest and consider its viability in times of fuel shortfalls.

3. Wind sites are less desirable but should be investigated. Wind electric turbines are noisy and require a lot of difficult maintenance, but in some cases where ground water is shallow or clean surface water is available, a windmill pumping to a high storage tank remains by far the most efficient and reliable means of storing and maintaining a pressurized water system. That is if and only if there is a regular occurrence of a good stiff breeze.

4. Roads where possible should be laid out as one way, single lane loops, with alternate means of emergency egress from the area. This design philosophy dramatically reduces the negative esthetic and noise pollution impact, and cost of road installation in rural and irregular topographies.

5. The boundary of the project should be fenced wherever easy 4-wheel drive, or ATV access is evident, solar powered electric is best and easy to install. The philosophy is not to create a fortress, which is impractical at these scales, but to discourage access for parties likely to commit burglary, hunt on private property, or simply show up unannounced and potentially threaten the peace and quiet of the neighborhood. If electric fencing is used take care to insure against fire hazard, such fences are often placed in very dry areas and can easily represent a powerful spark hazard.

6. Somewhere on the project or in a neighborhood conversion program there should be a central establishment that maintains food stores for emergency purposes, as well as a variety of larger tools for landscaping and maintenance purposes, available for rental by property owners on a no profit cooperative basis. Community grocery stores serve this purpose, but think about price gouging and the fact that most of these are sized to serve the largest possible area, which usually means everybody shops for a week of survival at the first sign of duress and the market's shelves are wiped out in one day. Remember, when chaos finally arrives a paper dollar and even a gold coin is not of much value to a starving renegade, or anybody else, but a candy bar or a bottle of whisky will last a long time in proper storage and may be

worth more than its weight in gold when the time comes. So stock your retreat as best you can, but remember to rotate perishables.

7. The local management corporation or neighborhood, should maintain at least one armed person, trained in CPR, on call at all times with vehicle that may be used as a default ambulance. That person's job will be to patrol for security enhancement, occasionally check empty homes when not in use, and generally be available to fill a variety of potential requests by property owners. This feature can be accomplished by a group of the homeowners willing to be trained and assume the responsibilities involved, as a kind of enhanced neighborhood watch program.

8. All projects and revised neighborhoods should incorporate a comprehensive set of covenants, conditions and restrictions deemed appropriate to the area and attached to the title of each individual parcel.

9. Each Project should include a site-specific management corporation designed so that the majority ownership of the sold out development specific corporation will accrue to the ownership of the parcel owners. Such localized corporations will be ultimately responsible for commonly pursued activities and enterprises, such as vineyards and wineries, stables, restaurants, commons management, golf courses, road maintenance, energy production etc.

10. Ongoing management and property maintenance fees may be required, but such immediate or potential responsibilities should be clearly spelled out in purchase contracts, and the nature or value of such obligations should not be changed after the fact except in the case of elective enterprise related too, but not directly attached to the title of the individual homes. In no case should failure to make such payments result in loss of property to individual purchasers, but instead accrue as a lien on the specific title of the property and due on sale or death. Conditions should not be allowed in which an evolving majority might decide to increase such fees for any arbitrary purpose such that poorer landowners might be forced to sell in order to meet such new obligations.

11. Each localized corporation should have at least two classes of stock; the first class rides with the title to the real property and cannot be divorced from it. The second class can be traded amongst the property owners as required. And where appropriate, the potential should be designed for a third class of stock available for both internal and external parties, and based on the potential evolving value of project owned enterprises.

As an example, a community co-operative project might include a fifty-acre vineyard and winery initially shared by and developed by the internal landowners. Growth of this enterprise might be hindered if restricted to internal ownership, but could potentially grow to a size that would allow the initial owners to essentially and eventually acquire and maintain their home sites for free or actually receive a profit from their investment without the need of sale. Such relational but independent profit venues must be designed to allow financial and growth venues in a secure but flexible structure that cannot endanger the security of the homeowner, in its home, from the outset.

Homes
Design Philosophy Specifications

1. Every home should have a basement of at least 400 sq. ft. or external root cellar. If basement, ideally, the ceiling of the basement should be framed of steel with steel decking. On the steel decking a slate or tile finish floor incorporating radiant hot water heating system should be installed. This type of system represents the strongest, most fire proof and most efficient heating system currently available and can now be performed at prices equivalent to less desirable systems. Such floors offer the most effective thermal mass resource for passive solar heating and cooling, and can be easily retrofitted to very effective hot water solar heating and or wood-bio fuel type systems. The mass of such floors in conjunction with the walled spaces above also offers an enhanced degree of protection from generalized nuclear fallout and chemical warfare conditions, and in conjunction with steel door access offers secure retreat at times of confrontation with undesirable elements. Further such systems are very strong without added expense, offering excellent tornado and storm protection, and excellent shelter in times of fire for both residents and their valuables. Each basement should have a basic bathroom, and wherever possible should be situated on a hillside *above* in ground septic. In locations such as Florida or other high water table areas, river flood plain and or tropical locations, look for a two story design with a first floor above ground consisting of concrete filled reinforced concrete block walls with minimal glazing to offer a near equivalent to a basement.

2. In areas subject to fire hazards, Homes should be finished on the exterior with a variety of materials and design proformas designed to offer as

nearly as possible a fire resistant exterior. In addition all homes should employ recognized fire defensive design and planting approaches in the landscaping around the immediate environs. Remember, when the oil runs out, it will be unlikely that any helicopters, or C41 Star-lifters, loaded with retardant, or state forestry fire engines and crews are going to show up and save your house. It will likely be up to you and your neighbors, and you are going to feel pretty damn silly, if you moved out the country to avoid the end of the world only to promptly watch your home burn down because you failed to do your homework.

3. Look for or incorporate intrinsic passive solar heating and cooling features, including thermal mass, enhanced insulation, convective ventilation, locally sized insolation control overhangs at appropriate glazing locations, etc.

4. Include a biomass alternative heating unit, i.e. high efficiency glass door, wood, coal or trash stove with heat recovery in the internal chimney piping. Look for one of these with a flat top that can be used for cooking. Be sure to clean your flue once a year at least.

5. Try to find a wood stove to cook on, to back up your gas range, they double as home heaters, and magically make your food taste great. If you live in a place where it gets hot in the summer, try an alternative to the old porch kitchen. Build the old porch kitchen with the wood cook stove, but super insulate the porch, and make insulated panels to cover the screened openings in the winter, then you can go on using your wood cooker all year long, with no excessive heat in the summer and no heat lost in the winter.

6. Health Inspectors will hate this, but as time goes on they will become more a part of the problem than a part of the solution, so wait until your house is finished and signed off. Pick a place at least a hundred feet from your well preferably downhill, not far from the house, in well-drained firm soil, preferably under a nice shade tree. Dig two holes, one about six to eight feet deep and about three feet in diameter, then one about four feet in diameter and three feet deep. Build yourself a nice vented outhouse over the deeper hole, and fill up the shallow hole with big gravel or small rocks, to about six inches from the top, place a galvanized screen over the top and finish filling the hole with small gravel, or un-grouted slate or flagstones, then hang a five gallon black plastic jug over the hole and insert a shower head. With a little basic plumbing you can hook this directly to your well or water storage tank and insert a couple of conveniently placed valves.

The drill for use is wet down, turn off, soap up, turn on, rinse off. During the spring, summer and fall, you will cut the water usage for two people from 200 gallons a day to about five gallons a day. If you have a standard 2500-gallon gravity water tank that you fill up by running your well's pump from a generator, that tank of water will last you an entire year, instead of the normal one-month. You will save a huge amount of electricity or gasoline and your pump might last a lifetime. With this kind of use, even if your pump fails you could convert to a hand pump, and the effort would be reasonable. With even a small amount of imagination and extra energy your outdoor bath can be a very pleasant addition to your lifestyle, and an interesting asset to your properties value.

Two commodities are important if you do this. 1. A supply of small chlorine swimming pool tablets for your water tank to keep it safe and clean. When you store these put the container in a thick sealed plastic bag, as the containers leak chlorine gas, which corrodes everything in the vicinity. 2. A good supply of bug spray, for spraying under the outhouse seat. In the old days one of the most common household fatalities occurred from spider bites acquired while on the John. It's a good bet spiders have less than adequate noses.

Empowerment of the Country Business

People who live and work in high-rise office buildings have for the most part always been a little nervous. Now their attitude is best exemplified by a secretary evacuated from the Sears Tower in Chicago as a precaution shortly after the WTC event. She said, in a voice quaking with undisguised fear; "I hate this building." As the world watched the twin towers pancake in massive catastrophic implosions, several salient truths became apparent.

1. No one will wholly trust the engineers and architects of such structures, who promise they are the safest places to be, and are essentially indestructible.

2. Insurance rates on high rises in compressed urban districts will escalate, as will just about all the other costs of doing business in such places.

3. In most of the developed world, infrastructures now in place, combined with lower labor, real estate, and virtually every other cost of business, except perhaps direct shipping means that it is now possible to conduct almost every

aspect of manufacturing and business in rural, country, or suburban locations with little or no loss of business advantage.

Historically, the main reason people decided to live in urban locations was the availability of good employment. The axiom is that urban people are rich while country folks are poor. Therefore developers in the country tended to develop what were essentially low-income housing projects, or land speculation projects with no housing at all. Urban dwellers bragged their quality of life was better because of the opera, the plays and fine restaurants, but nowadays most people prefer satellite based home entertainment systems, and virtually every rural resort destination is capable of boasting at least three, four-star-restaurants. While few would debate the argument that it's better to have a few deer nibbling your flowers, than a few junkies shooting up in your front yard, or broken glass falling out of the sky.

So, historically the quality of life in the country is higher, but the employment opportunities less enriching. Now, there is little justification for businesses to demand locations in urban centers. Therefore it seems obvious that it's up to the country developers to think about creating conditions that will encourage business to relocate, and for business developers to consider new locations and comprehensive relocation plans towards the country. The Internet empowered the work anywhere generation, the natural evolution is to provide the everywhere else for the Internet generation to work.

As a result it now makes sense for country developers and small town administrators to consider and support business-oriented projects. This concept goes beyond the idea of direct land related enterprises such as agriculture and vacation. Ask yourself, what is the modern day justification for a moderately sized manufacturer of wilderness sporting goods to be located in the urban center of downtown Seattle? The answer is, there is none. The kind of people that work in such an enterprise, the image of the company, the working conditions, the cost of living, the quality of life for everyone involved is dramatically advantaged by relocation to the country, if the country is able to provide the constructed environment conducive for the enterprise. In the Author's little town there is a major employer who makes dental equipment, their factory is way the hell and gone up the mountain and out in the woods, but they are doing just fine.

It should be noted that it has been a common habit of moderate to large businesses to establish recreational retreat properties, which serve as perks or rewards for employees, as retreats for seminars, think tank sessions, and for strategy and marketing purposes. Enhancing these existing proformas with advantages discussed, especially the directed potentials for the projects to generate independent income as well as status, in today's nervous political and social environment, makes the decision a simple one for most corporate executives with any capital flexibility at all.

The President of the United States and his heads of state now conduct much of their business in Camp David or from a ranch in the remote wilds of Texas. If America can be run from a wilderness installation, it becomes reasonable to assume most of the lesser institutions it supports can also be run from such locations with equal advantage and prestige.

Relational Enterprises
The Aquaculture Vineyard and Winery

Vineyard land in California is an immensely powerful and valuable attraction for prospective country property buyers. The typical selling price for planted land in the four county prime grape region is $500,000.00 per acre, this is an outrageous figure as the crop value of the grapes that acre can produce is a maximum of $5,000 per season. People pay hugely for the prestige. As a result areas previously considered marginal vineyard districts are slowly being developed.

Vineyards are labor intensive, but perhaps 60% of that labor is sublimely enjoyable, the ultimate retirement occupation, and many happy folks might say the all around highest and best use for a five-acre parcel. Because there are certain periods of intense activity interspersed with long periods of almost no activity, the typical maximum area of vineyard a couple can maintain on their own is about four acres. Because of the relatively low value of the unprocessed grapes, it's nearly impossible to pay for labor and break even at this scale.

The money in grapes is in the winery. A typical bottle costs three dollars to produce, including winery overhead, capitalization, bottles and the grapes. That is if you can avoid paying half a million an acre for the land. It retails out of the boutiques at avg. $21.00. But a small winery costs about $300,000.00 and cannot be supported by the typical single-family vineyard. You need a minimum vineyard of about twenty acres and forty is better.

Now imagine a typical country subdivision of about 24 parcels with a density of five acres per site. If the individual lots are haphazardly developed as vineyards the resale value goes way up but the buyer satisfaction is almost always reduced to frustration and anger. However if the private area per site is three acres and the good cropland is in common vineyard, you get 48 acres in one operation, which is a significant basis for a significant boutique winery. That winery, when supported by an adequate crop is a business that can be commercially financed by the property owners or a relational corporation.

Owning a parcel or home site that participates directly in such an enterprise becomes a remarkably desirable and financially rewarding asset for everyone from all directions. Shares tied to the parcels own the vineyard and owners can provide labor, which is credited against the corporation's profits on an hourly basis, or paid directly. Those proceeds can then go back to their mortgage until paid or accrue in any way that makes sense. The owners also get home sites oriented to common vineyards, a sublime esthetic, and lots of elegant wines to impress their guests with. It also works as a profile to retrofit existing wineries and vineyards with low density housing projects, and there are a lot of these that are marginally profitable that can be purchased and re-purposed at significant advantage.

Wineries are intensely used about three months each year and sit idle the rest of the time. However, one thing not commonly known or advantaged is that with a few minor alterations a winery can be made into a brewery. Further that such an installation can be enhanced with a still and it becomes a place you can make any variety of alcoholic beverage including high profit exotic liqueurs, and fuel alcohol. Thus the assets of a typical winery can be enhanced and employed year round producing a variety of products, which reduces the carry and increases profitability.

An aquaculture farm is a similar enterprise. It takes less land, but it takes water. Wastewater from a fish farm is full of nutrients. Treated wastewater from a fish farm is within pathogen levels low enough to use for drip system irrigation of vineyards. Most vineyard irrigation systems are designed with booster pumps coming from tank storage fed by wells. And all drip systems have to have screen filtration.

The technology for on-land aquaculture is now well proven. This type of aquaculture especially in the salmon, tilapia and trout rearing operations can be highly profitable and analysis of a particular site's profitability is now streamlined to a moderately simple set of factors, further the synergies inherent in a combined aquaculture vineyard installation go well beyond the

known fact that smoked salmon and dill trout go great with good beer and wine.
Typically the capital costs and operational requirements of an economically viable fish farm are larger than those that can be handled by a typical couple or home farmer, but they are easily within the means of a cooperative organization sponsored by 24 families.

Small dairies: A single milk cow produces more milk products than a single family can use, while eight or so milk cows which must be bred every year with either beef or milk bulls can produce enough milk products and beef for 24 families per annum. That includes cheese, cream, sour cream, milk, steak, burgers etc. What is the typical food served with wine, Cheese and apples.

Orchard: A single-family orchard is generally not very profitable because an orchard large enough to be viable demands labor hiring and tools and supplies larger than can be justified by one family. But a commonly owned orchard can use commonly owned tools and supplies and the efficiencies and increased manpower allows the operation to become viable. There are your apples.

Wood lots: Wood lots add more than just esthetic greenbelt. A cord of firewood costs about $200 in the country, and is going to increase in value dramatically as the oil and gas goes away. If efficiently used in a passive solar home it can replace $600 or more in alternate fuel heating bills. That value is further increased if harvested by the user as no tax is paid on the purchase income. Firewood also increases national security by reducing the amount of imported oil, and a good supply insures warm winters even if that imported supply is curtailed or dramatically inflated.

Nurseries: Since these projects are located in the country. Agriculture related nurseries are an excellent venue. Grapes are propagated from waste cuttings. Orchard from grafted seed stock. These are also regimes that require some enjoyable labor and occasional care and can be done close to homes by homeowners.

Home site gardens, orchards and chickens: The typical homestead food self sufficiency regimes under current conditions are difficult to justify as the labor involved is usually higher than that which can be earned in normal occupations and then spent on retail produce, and a single home's production is usually not sufficient to warrant marketability and income return venues. However, 24 home sites working co-operative country gardens and maintaining independent, chicken-rabbit sheds can easily produce enough product to keep a significant country market stocked and turning a significant profit throughout the season. In fact such a production, combined with cooperative meat production including elk, beef, chicken, rabbit, venison, pork, and of course salmon and trout is in some cases sufficient to form the foundational basis of a country town super market's supply base.

Country Store: Such a store may be combined with hardware, and self sufficiency supplies, feed and vet supply, and outlet for co-op wine, beer and liqueurs and it becomes a powerful and unique retail anchor outlet for co-op produce when combined with output from other local farmers. Such a store also becomes important in that it offers justification, actuality and wholesale purchasing power to the co-op owners as a powerful resource for the co-op in times of duress, and as a locally sustaining and socially reinforcing resource to the general local community. Something that also becomes critical in times of social and economic duress.

Energy co-ops: Localized energy production co-ops are the way of the future, especially in rural areas. Localized energy co-ops enjoy a variety of venues and efficiencies not available to the large classical producers. These include multiple fuel gasifiers and pyrolysis, bio mass co-generation, and methane and ethanol production units located close to agricultural production areas. Localized use of wind and hydro. Such co-ops can dramatically enhance the security and enjoyment of life for locals, but also represent powerful venues for enhancing national security and economic health by reducing demand for imported fuels, enhancing capacity of large systems by lowering demand profiles and increasing peak resource availability, reducing overall impact of terrorist and wartime vulnerability to the centralized grid, and create significantly improved delivery efficiencies by reducing electricity travel distance and thus resistance losses across delivery lines. Local energy co-ops also dramatically enhance income venues for co-op participants by reducing participant's costs of energy plus cost of taxable income needed to purchase energy. They also allow use of waste raw materials and local resources to be converted to significant profits through very high profit sales to the national grid at peak usage rates

Co-op large tool rental: One of the major costs of owning maintaining and operating a country home site, homestead and or small agricultural installation is the need for purchasing and maintaining a significant array of expensive tools, which in most cases simply sit in sheds unused for most of the year and which represent a major irritation to the average home user as they demand constant maintenance and repair. Also the initial cost of such tools often discourages the average local property owner from pursuing a variety of land based income venues it might otherwise enjoy. The normal solution to this problem is rental from a for profit store. However, as anyone who has used a tool rental store will recognize, such stores typically operate according to one of the highest profit margins in the country. Often set so that three to five rentals will pay for the capital cost of a tool However a co-op representing the capital power of say 24 homes can purchase most of the tools needed to empower its participants at clearly significant savings to the end users. Co-op owners get to use the tools at cost, subsidized by for profit rentals to the general community, which in most cases means such tools become essentially free to the co-op owners and potentially offer yet another venue for profit.

Out of a group of 50 individuals there will always be at least one person who is mechanically inclined. Such a person not only enjoys working with and maintaining the machines, but also automatically inherits an important and respected position in the community while enjoying a local venue of employment. When translated to the home-co-op based enhanced land use productivity these tools allow, the economic benefits dramatically escalate to the co-op community as a whole. Such a co-operative establishment is then able to grow into a variety of material purchasing venues based on the same structure. Building Materials, agricultural supplies, pharmaceuticals, are just a few. If these venues are established at a general commercial enterprise located in the development's host small town and combined with the co-op super market-hardware mentioned, they represent a dramatically enhanced 21st century general store, or country style one stop shopping mall style establishment.

Fishing Co-ops: Ocean oriented projects could purchase a fishing boat and enjoy the benefits of the co-operative approach.

This co-operative approach to country living is not new, and the advantages have been thoroughly proven over time, but historically its usages have been limited to various segregated small enterprise aspects. By providing a residential anchoring community, prepared from the outset to evolve towards a comprehensive set of co-operative community enterprises such proformas become dramatically empowered.

The list of potential enterprises that can grow from this relational level is essentially limited only by the aspirations and energies of the co-op participants

Co-Op Residential Farms

Old farms exist all over the country in areas near but removed from urban suburban locations, often owned by families struggling against overwhelming conditions to stay afloat and keep their heritage within the family. Many such farms are located adjacent to prime riverside locations because rivers produce the prime bottomland best for agriculture. Often the farm's home site and agricultural-animal husbandry improvements are located well away from these idyllic riverside locations because of the potential for flooding and the limitations of classical architectures. However modern construction techniques based on concrete and pressure treated wood pole foundations when applied to strictly residential development can allow safe and secure development of these highly desirable riverside locations with little or no additional expense over standard on ground foundations. In most cases such foundations will qualify for federal flood plain insurance, which is demanded by the funding agencies in such situations. Many large farms also contain other underutilized marginally productive areas, such as high ground forested areas, ideal for view sites, and hilltops unsuited for farming.

Such farms often end up being sold as a result of forced conditions to normal developers who chop them up and install high density subdivisions, or when local planning conditions forbid, they are often lost and fall out of productivity to become derelict farmland of little value other than pleasant countryside for travelers passing by on nearby freeways, something that may become rare.

A typical 300-acre farm might have a river front area perfect for an idyllic project of 30 homes on 1 to 3 acre parcels. If such homes are carefully sited amongst the trees normal along such locations they have little or no visual impact on the countryside and result in little or no destruction of productive farmland. By setting aside the original farmstead and a good chunk of surrounding land and maintaining the original owner as a major shareholder in the Co-Op project corporation, and placing all the productive land into common ownership, the farmer can realize a significant boost in cash available for direct enhancement of its lifestyle. It may also enjoy curing of all the liens endangering its property, and will be able to maintain its lifestyle and productive skills on exactly the same land from its family home. The farmer also enjoys a new population of associates all concerned with the productive preservation of the farm and the extended advantages of cooperative potentials. Such projects can often win approval of local planning agencies and communities on agriculturally zoned land, precisely because the productive value of the land is both preserved and enhanced through permanent non-development agreements at the time of rezoning across the productive area of the farm, and because previously unproductive low tax yield lands are converted to taxable income producing properties with little or no adverse environmental or esthetic impact on the general area.

With the new availability of a much larger population of people interested in enhancing the beauty and productivity of the farm, diversification of the farm's productivity venues suddenly becomes feasible, and there will in many cases be an organic evolution away from strictly monoculture style cropping to increasing blocks of orchard and berry production, diversification of cash cropping, better management of woodlot resources and increased venues for protein production through aquaculture. There will also be a natural tendency to minimize artificial fertilizer and pesticide use.

If several such projects are performed in the environs of a country town, they serve to justify establishment of the community co-op store mentioned earlier, and this outlet serves as an additional retail option for the various farm's products, which then naturally enjoy an incentive towards further diversification towards a wider selection of salable local produce. With such an approach residential development in rural areas actually works to enhance and preserve the productive and esthetic values of underutilized farm properties and thus is a win for all involved; in the project itself, and in the greater community.

Ben knew there was fresh wheat flour on the island from the recent visit of the Maranatha Maru, and he was looking forward to dipping a rare and expensive Baguette, 'maybe even' he thought 'a Brioche' in his coffee, at the Tevaville Boulangerie before he caught the first Le Truck into Faa'a early that morning on his way back to work.

Tevaville was a post fall village that had grown out from the old Restaurant Gauguin across the coconut shaded park towards Cooks Bay, and filled in the space behind right up to the Botanical Gardens.

There were now a couple of long and very busy floating piers running out into Cooks bay, with lots of small boats tied up; their owners already bringing in the previous nights catch. A couple of baskets full of reef lobsters caught his eye and he decided there and then to take the second bus, and treat himself to a fire roasted tail as well.

'Besides' Ben thought to himself ' I like it here, and I am after all nearly a chief? Hmmm?' He felt his feet, quite of their own accord moving out from under him as they decided to follow those baskets of lobsters towards their quickly arriving destiny.

To Ben's credit Tevaville was a very nice place to be, unlike Papea'ete and Faa'a it had been entirely built after the 'fall' out of local materials, and there were almost none of the dilapidated old western style buildings around. No big streets full of potholes, just soft paths of coconut frond snaking between the skelter of surprisingly sophisticated and often richly finished thatch homes and small store fronts. To a westerner from our time it would have felt exotic indeed, but to Ben it just felt like home.

Chapter Ten
Arcadian Village Communities

Aside from writing strange books like this one, one of the Author's primary occupations resides in designing planning and consulting for self-sufficient resort communities. As a result there is a certain personal poignancy in the realization that one of the effects of the end of the fossil fuel world will be the end of quick international travel for all but the truly super-rich, which means the day of the exotic resort may be about to close.

Nevertheless, the Self Sufficient Eco Resort planning model intrinsically mandates a number of features that makes it about as close to the transition and post fossil fuel ideal evolution of the Arcadian village that we can find.

Many SSERs are built by well to do individuals who possess a the key Arcadian trait of altruistic self interest, their projects are sometimes built not with the primary idea of making their owner, or a distant group of investors rich, but for the purpose of providing an alternative means of earning income for local populations in remote areas. Thus the transient resort engine is an alternative means to justify better housing, disposable income and the installation and maintenance of self-sufficiency infrastructures for native populations.

SSER's are often located in remote areas far away from energy grids, infrastructures and easy supplies, which is why they need to be as self sufficient as possible. As the world evolves towards transitional collapse it's likely the function and value of SSER's will evolve away from transient hospitality, towards security retreats, and as a result will most likely become the core structures of new self sufficient communities able to weather most arriving conditions precisely because of their remote locations, their inherent self-sufficiency and close relationship to local natural resources.

As a result it's likely, that the development of evolved SSER's as Co-Operatively owned and operated Self Sufficient Security Retreats will actually experience a significant increase. COSSSR's are an evolution of the remote rural co-operatives discussed above, but can be thought of as infrastructure, tool, and housing packages which can be applied to any suitable location anywhere on the planet, including retrofits for existing remote villages. To be clear, this office and a few others like it, can consult on ideal locations, survey the geomorphologies of the site, design a comprehensive self sufficiency infrastructure package, along with a variety of appropriate housing regimes, arrange-purchase all the requisite materials, pack them into shipping containers and ship them just about anywhere in the world. Then offer onsite development management using local labor.

Remember, without the massive fossil fuel energy subsidy that drives the developed world, the developed world will most likely collapse, then eventually, if any aspect of that society survives, and or no massive energy miracle arrives, human society in general will most likely come to resemble those human societies now and historically in the world that have existed in a more or less stable state since the beginning of time without the massive fossil fuel subsidy.

Examples of these still in the world include, rural villages in China and India, island villages and small towns, frontier America in the Seventeen Hundreds. In fact the whole world will be sent back to the Seventeen Hundreds and before. There are two major differences. The first is that the population of the planet is way over what it was then, and the second is technology.

It's likely the collapse of the energy structure and possibly the climate changes expected will dramatically reduce the population over the next couple of hundred years, it's also likely that for most of the planet's societies, these times will be horrendous in nature. As a result the best places to be will be areas that are remote, lightly populated, and blessed with sufficient natural resources or conditions conducive to survival and self-sufficiency. Given the high probability of the arriving conditions it seems clear that it would be a constructive thing both at an individual or personal level for participants, and at a larger social level, for the future in general if as many such COSSSR's were developed in as many possible alternative locations now.

When we think of a typical eco resort, we tend to think of thatch huts in tropical paradise, or pole platforms in jungles, while in many ways these are appropriate, the real purpose of COSSSR's is to provide for long term self sufficiency and a reasonably comfortable level of alternative lifestyle for the permanent inhabitants. A lifestyle that can go on in relatively unhindered fashion while the rest of the world falls flat on its face, a lifestyle and social structure that can survive intact for the possibly two hundred years of transition and beyond, preserving the good and important aspects of human society through that period of duress and then allow the re-colonization of the planet in a civilized fashion, after the fall.

This sounds like radical thinking, and we can only hope it is, however, the indicators are all to real, and the lessons we can learn by exploring the concepts and necessary technologies can be applied to life and social structures in general with positive results.

Five primary factors form the foundations of the COSSSR concept; the village, population density, alternative energy resources, the capacity to produce or acquire food locally, and reasonable geomorphologies.

The Village

For the nearly ten thousand years prior to the industrial revolution the agrarian village social structure has been the preferred vehicle of daily life for the majority of the human race. A village is a clustering of individual family units usually between 50 and 1500 people, which may serve an extended rural population of about 300 to 3,000 additional folks who are usually engaged in local agrarian or other food or energy producing activities. The purpose of the cluster is to provide a social and economic focus, central more defensible facilities for food storage, and justification for needed basic services, like blacksmiths-hardware dealers, markets and such.

A village is a relatively small group of people working *together* to achieve efficiencies of survival and comfort that are much more difficult for individual families to achieve. The size of a *successful* village is usually determined by the maximum number of souls the village can support by working or advantaging the local lands that comprise the environs of the village. In just about every country on the planet, except for America, the village remains the preferred *rural* social structure. In the post fossil fuel world even America will witness a return to village societies as a rural structure.

In small villages, everyone knows and immediately recognizes everyone else. This simple fact has remarkably healthy social consequences. In such an environment burglars and other miscreants cannot operate successfully, so police, lawyers, and judges are largely not required. A person quickly finds its reputation based on its actions to be a publicly defined thing, so the quality of its work, and the level of its acceptable social conduct automatically improve. In addition, over time such villages function rather like extended families, meaning people come to genuinely care for each other. Children are safer and more easily cared for, as are the elderly, and those who are down on their luck poor or hungry.

The concept of the village need not be limited to rural areas, but can be retrofitted over existing neighborhoods, both suburban and urban. It's simply a matter of defining appropriate boundaries and then initiating localized village or neighborhood meetings on a regular basis, for the purposes of enhancing the lives of the inhabitants at a locally personal level. Urban and suburban villages can initiate co-operative gardens, purchase goods co-operatively in bulk, maintain neighborhood watch and patrol agencies, participate in very local energy production co-ops and enjoy a host of other advantages not available through impersonal, inefficient and otherwise ineffective larger government bodies. In the post fossil fuel world, the rural village will be the preferred social structure, because comfortable survival can be assured with the minimum consumption of artificial energy resources.

In arable rural land areas, the ideal minimum ratio of open or agricultural land, to developed village land is about 1 in 5. In other words out of a 200 acre piece of undeveloped land, 40 acres should be for village, and 160 for agricultural use. A typical village of single family homes with basic communal facilities, things like equipment barns, food storage and processing sheds for three to five hundred can be easily developed in an area of about twenty to forty acres, meaning the minimum agricultural village development would require only a hundred twenty to two hundred or so acres of good land. In areas where the land is poor these figures can go way up, and care and expertise is required to make this judgment successfully.

The villages should be located centrally in their attendant areas of agricultural lands, on high ground if practical. The farm plots should not be large monoculture tracts, but instead small plots averaging about two to five acres, best delineated by hedgerows, wild strips or canals. In the plots, agricultural variety should be encouraged. There is nothing new about such a scheme. In fact it was, and in many places remains the typical landscape of countries that have enjoyed long term, sustained civilization the world over. It can be found in such diverse locations as the wine country of France, the foothills of northern Italy, the countryside of Indonesia, across most of China, and in it's ultimate state of the art, the intensely developed highly productive countryside of Japan. Where small family villages remain to this day surrounded by privately held intensely cultivated plots that seldom exceed four acres. In Japan, one family typically farms one plot, with pride, and that plot often produces crops with an annual value in excess of $60,000 U.S.

These smaller plots are important as they allow crop diversity, which means production can be handled without huge tractors and most importantly insects, diseases and bad climate years find it harder to destroy all the produce. Remember, after the fall artificial fertilizers and pesticides will in most areas be hard to come by and very expensive.

One of the pitfalls of small farm plots is the high cost of the tools required to make such projects work. Again, this is where Co-Operation is critical. While it's important for the land you work to be your own, so that you can directly enjoy the rewards of your labor, it's not so important to own your own tools. A village can buy these major investments together, use and maintain them, in cooperative fashion.

In laying out the villages minimize through roads, keep the roads small, and unpaved. In the post fossil fuel world there will be no asphalt to patch potholes, no concrete trucks, no cars as such. The likeliest forms of transport will be the multi-purpose tractor that runs on locally obtained bio-fuels and converts them to gas. These were commonly known as Gazogenes in the 1930's and 40's. There will also likely be small electric carts; wide tired bicycles, tricycles, horses, oxen, lamas, feet, and a few small trucks powered by ethanol and other bio fuels. As a result, road sizes and engineering can be downscaled almost to a path level, about 1.5 meters wide per lane. With one-way roads (single lanes) encouraged wherever practical. Such roads can be paved with gravel. At this size the overall negative impact of roadways on the general countryside is magically curtailed, yet it remains possible for large trucks traveling slowly to use them.

Villages placed in areas subject to flooding, which will be common as flood plain is also the richest long-term non fossil fuel fertilizer subsidized farmland, can be built entirely on pole foundations and most of the main floors raised a couple meters above grade, buildings can be connected by inexpensive bridges and decks. By using a combination of modern structural systems, and locally obtained materials, buildings can enjoy long safe lifetimes while remaining inexpensive to produce, and blending well into the surrounding environment.

The reader is skeptical at this point. 'This guy thinks I'm going to give up my 2,700 sq. ft. tract home, move to some God forsaken corner of the earth and live in some twisted commune, in a hut, must be some kind of old hippy?'

By 2011 your skepticism will likely be tempered by desperation, and by then it will be to late to seek real alternatives. The Author has a big house in the country, and might have a hard time giving it up and moving to a remote village, but it's also true that a big house, new car and giant T.V. do not necessarily define lifestyle happiness. A large part of a big house is about maintaining that house and it's grounds, and in paying for it, and the truth is only about 900 of the 3,000 sq. feet of the Author's house is really utilized or important to productivity and the important things of daily life. He also remembers two years from his youth spent in an army tent with a plywood floor and wood cook stove at a cattle camp in the high mountains of Idaho, as some of the happiest of his life.

Plenty of good food, a little wine or beer, a loving mate, a wealth of good friends, and a healthy and productive local environment are the real things that define a potentially happy and fulfilling life. The rest of it is for insecure egos and fools like us. Most of the native populations of Polynesia are now highly educated and reasonably sophisticated, but continue to live in homes not far removed from their ancestors thatch huts. They spend most of their lives outside close to nature, and it's a fact that there is no other society on earth that is as a general rule, happier than these.

The suggested village structure offered here is not offered as an old hippies commune, but as a tiny town of private homes, where friends with similar goals help each other to accomplish the basic necessities of life in a long term self sustaining social structure.

It's important to remember that unlike the old hippy communes, if a group of fifty or so contemporary families decided to 'drop out' now in anticipation of the future, and establish a co-operative village in some remote near paradisiacal location, they would be able to realize through the liquidation or manipulation of their probable combined assets, a very significant block of development capital. This means the new village of smaller homes might very likely include a host of state of the art features, which could make the resulting new lifestyle, a very enjoyable and satisfying long-term alternative.

Population Density

The key to success resides in being able to control the population of a given area of land, so that the land can continue to support the resident population without long distance subsidies of energy and goods, effectively forever. If the village is located in an area of rich productive farmland and Bio-dynamic or Permaculture techniques (To be discussed later) are applied to the agricultural regimes, it becomes a fairly easy task to define the ideal population for a given ratio of necessary lands, keeping in mind some room for unavoidable growth and some consideration for bad climate and seasons. It's also critically important to include sufficient area for sustainable production of bio-fuels produce, which can include carefully, managed woodlots-forest, hedgerows, or oil crops.

Such projects might also be developed as second home co-operative projects, that might be partially financed through employment as managed resort accommodations. For that reason and others, many such projects might be located in areas of dramatic natural appeal, but lesser practical appeal in terms of land productivity. If this occurs it's important to consider the value of adjacent or nearby wild or common lands for their ability to produce protein and other resources. Keep in mind that a forest that seems filled with deer right now will be challenged dramatically when those deer become a primary source of protein, so if you are banking on something like this, make sure the wild areas are really big, national forest big, or rugged ocean coastline big.

The second issue concerning population resides in avoiding large external quantities of it. While you most likely will not want to divorce yourself entirely from the world, you do want to anticipate those hungry hoards from the cities, and locate so that such encounters will be minimized. This means use those roads less traveled whenever possible, and the *best* locations are those that can only be accessed by boat, or that are truly remote. Avoid locations that are well known as retreat or survival areas like those million dollar movie star ranches in Montana, such places will be targets to the long distance enabled gangs. The Author's favorite areas as you probably already guessed include the outer high islands of Polynesia, but also the Inside Passage along the British Columbia Coast, Islands in the Mediterranean, valleys and hills in the Ozarks and Appalachians, rural wet areas of Spain, (they do exist) and perhaps most surprisingly the Eastern Foothills of the

Andes in Bolivia, along with many others. We will address the issue of areas in greater detail later on. A good rule of thumb is to look for very large areas with low populations, stable decent climate and lots of undeveloped land, then focus on smaller areas within these domains that offer positive local geomorphologies.

Alternative Energy Resources

No matter how good they are technically, solar panels only work when the sun is out, and wind turbines only turn when the wind is blowing which is also seldom at night. Batteries quickly wear out and using electricity to store energy in variations of physical batteries, things like pumping water uphill for storage are expensive complex and inherently inefficient. There really is only one ideal long-term self-sustaining source for electrical generation, hydropower. So if you like the things electricity allows, you should locate your village or retreat near running water. Modern technologies allow electrical generation from flat streams with strong currents, small pools with significant height and other configurations, but make sure the water is reasonably under control, and build your system as strong as you possibly can and then stronger. Above all keep the technology as simple as possible, and keep all the spare parts you can someplace else in dry and sealed conditions. You can consider plugging into the grid if one exists in your chosen location, especially if there is a local area co-op based on a good sized hydro facility in the area, energy generation efficiency dramatically benefits from increasing factors of scale. Keep in mind; most island communities right now exist on diesel or oil-fired generators that are often turned off at night. If this is the case you might consider becoming active in the community and encouraging the development of micro hydro opportunities usually abundant on high islands.

Coconut oil can be converted to bio-diesel, but not enough for generators, keep this for lamps, and tractors, boats and cooking. In the high mountains bio oil is precious and hard to come by so you need lots of wood and gasifiers to fill this role. The point here is that you have to look carefully for these kinds of resources, think about how hard and expensive it will be to harness them, how long and how reliable will the technologies needed be, before you chose an area to relocate.

Food

The Author spent four very enjoyable years in a small town on the Mendocino Coast of California. Maybe it's the advent of age, maybe too much wine for too many evenings past, but try as he might he can only remember one trip in all that time to the Big Supermarket in Fort Bragg. But he certainly does remember an endless cycle of very enjoyable evenings pursuing a regular habit of collecting mussels and sea urchins, or sitting on a favorite rock slightly above the waves catching several sea trout or the occasional big Grouper for dinner, in an enjoyable half hour, or harvesting the potatoes and blackberries from the backyard.

With his friends in the Islands, life was similar, every night we would dive off the back porch into the lagoon for a refreshing swim and a little spear fishing. If you do your homework, certain areas near the ocean are by far the easiest places to live a long life with little worry about starving no matter what condition the rest of the world finds itself in. His extended time in Idaho was similar, two years spent helping a family of six homestead a large wilderness property, living on not much more than twenty dollars a week, and most of that spent on Canadian Whisky and ubiquitous sacks of rolling tobacco, food came from the land, from the cows, from the forests and streams, and it was never more plentiful, more varied or more thoroughly enjoyed. You can have this too, if you do your homework before you move.

Of course in a transition and post fossil fuel world, everyone will not be so lucky and most who survive will find themselves in small agricultural communities. In such cases the food will have to be created. The most efficient methods for long term productivity can be found in Mr. Bill Mollison's books concerning the genre of agriculture he single handedly created called Permaculture. Get these books and study them, then apply the principles to the land around your village at the very beginning of development. Within these designs, locate a community garden and apply the methods of John Jeavons and other like minded individuals who have explored the variations of what is commonly known as French Bio-Dynamic gardening. For each family of four in the village you will need an intensely gardened area for eating corn, beans vegetables and such of about half an acre.

Then about four acres employed in larger agricultures, these larger plots can be co-operatively or privately worked, but the total yield of the village lands needs to be coordinated at town meetings.

Folks in tropical areas have this figured out the good way, instead of planting useless lawns they stick, fei, oranges and grapefruits, avocados, breadfruit, and similar productive trees wily nilly all about the yard, then just pick whatever's handy to supplement the days catch. Then there are usually a few folks who specialize in taro and sweet potatoes.

Bees have endured a bad reputation lately as a result of the advent of the African Killers, but the truth is the African species is having less of a real impact than the media would have you believe, and it's also a fact that even though a lot more caution is required, the African bees can be domesticated and can produce significantly more honey than the normal European varieties. Regardless, right now because of the oil economy sugar has turned sweetness into something taken for granted, on the other side of the transition, for folks living in northern latitudes it will be a rare and precious commodity and will more likely be available only from beets and honey. Bees enhance the environment, make it more productive and yield honey and wax. Even now, as a specialty crop bees and honey are a very profitable business.

Local Geomorphologies

Fresh water, fresh water, fresh water, there is a legitimate debate going on right now as to which will start the first wars of resource imperialism, fresh water or oil. The good news about water is that unlike oil, fresh water renews itself. The preferred fresh water resource for the post fossil fuel world is of course quickly flowing water because that provides electricity, easy irrigation, and is the best self-cleaning surface water. Flowing fresh water can be channeled into tanks for aquaculture, which is the most efficient method of producing animal protein, without the need for pumps, and effluent released directly onto crops.

Forget desalinization as an alternative, forget deep wells, if you do choose to settle near a lake, try to pick one that enjoys a good bit of wind on a regular basis, and you can outfit your village with wind pumps and gravity tanks efficiently. If you do choose to settle near the ocean you still need fresh water, even if it rains every day, be careful, cisterns get polluted, and with changing climates your rain might dry up.

Do not pick a deserted atoll, no matter how much it resembles a romantic paradise, food varieties are very limited, as is fresh water, and it could be under the sea in a few years. However, high islands in the Mediterranean area, even if they appear to be fairly dry right now will more than likely enjoy a wetter climate in coming years. Twelve thousand years ago when the ice still covered much of Europe, the Saharan desert was a Garden of Eden pocked with lakes and numerous rivers, and the Sphinx was getting drenched with regular rain. Don't take this as a recommendation to buy cheap property in the Sahara, but the odds are the climate in the Med will moderate, and life on its islands can be pleasant even now.

Trees trees and more trees, trees are fuel, food, trap the rain, moderate the climate and provide ideal domain for wild and grazing animals. As soon as you get moved in plant trees that grow fast, trees that bear nuts, trees that bear fruit.

Look for areas of good soil, it is important to test the soil for PH, Nitrogen, Potash and Potassium, even with a rich natural flora the soil can be deceptive and may need correction if you are planning on practicing productive agriculture. You will need to make those corrections before the oil runs out, as after that complete fertilizers will be very hard to come by.

Above all use common sense, think study and do your homework before you settle on a location, think about changing conditions of climate in the future.

In recent history the development of remote locations has often been remarkably expensive. Installing improvements that must be self-sufficient, yet capable of offering a level of amenity acceptable to the pampered middle class citizen of the developed world is a difficult task. But modern technologies and new construction approaches are beginning to deliver a variety of tools that promise to allow success at reasonable cost.

Architecture

Architecture suffers when existing appropriate vernaculars of style are ignored in favor of pure form follows function solutions, price point ratios, or the usually twisted attempts at creativity that result when architects ignore everyone else's best interests in an effort to further their careers through their own 'unique' styles. *'Culture is always the best architect.'* Meaning those vernaculars which have evolved in a particular geographical climate and cultural domain over sometimes thousands of years will always be more satisfying esthetically and environmentally than say a 'technically sophisticated' imported style created out of someone's imagination on the sterilized thirtieth floor of a skyscraper in New York.

This overall philosophy does not preclude creativity, originality, or the application of state of the art technologies. Instead it demands that a particular area will be best-developed using vernaculars proven over long periods of time to be appropriate to local climate and esthetics. Which thankfully usually means maximum use of local readily available materials. One can borrow various elements from similar climates and geographies located in distant parts of the globe and use them to blend in and accent a local style. For instance, an all natural wood pole structure in a steep British Columbia coastal canyon, might have elements of style drawn from Japanese coastal villages of the 1600's combined with Viking elements from 900, combined with coastal Amerindian motifs, tricked out with a few accents drawn from the pure imaginations of sophisticated computer game world architects. Lights and other fixtures can draw from the Art Deco or Craftsman period without conflict.

Such a structure can seem to have been in its ultimate location for thousands of years and thus be entirely esthetically and environmentally appropriate. But it will at the same time immediately invoke a sense of something exotic.

Obviously, in the arriving times the real cost of a home that requires less energy to accomplish it's purposes will be less than that of an energy guzzler, and six thousand square feet of bedrooms that you can't afford to heat are not of much real value. However, active solar heating systems are inherently complex will break down and depreciate quickly. The key features to look for are insulation, and thermal mass. You can't get too much insulation and unless your roof leaks it's hard to screw this part up. Thermal mass however, can be a problem. Thermal mass does not automatically provide heat, it stores heat, but it also stores cold. As a result if a contractor tells you that concrete slab is passive solar heating, but the house has almost no windows facing the sun to heat the slab and the perimeter of the slab is not carefully insulated, your house will always be cold unless you pump in huge amounts of heat to heat up the slab. Thermal mass only stores ambient or applied energy and then releases it over time. That means if you have thermal mass and you open your windows at night and let the house get cold, then close it up in the morning for most of the day your house will be naturally cool, while if your mass gets a lot of solar input or is heated naturally during the day, and you close up your house at night the house will be warmer. You have to use care with how it is installed and in most cases take care of it every day to make it work properly.

Zoning, remember the folks in Vermont. Look at the layout of the house, if it comes to it, can you close off much of the house and keep warm in the living room and kitchen?

In the northern hemisphere major glazing should be facing south, southeast, southwest, regardless of view, you can retrofit by filling in north windows or replacing them with smaller ones, and if you get cooked in the summer hire a local contractor to install properly sized insolation overhangs above your southern windows.

Hang thick curtains and if you can install Velcro along the edges and bottom, then you can seal up the windows at night. Look into well-based heat exchangers, these can be very efficient in certain areas, but keep it as simple as possible and do careful financial return calculations, as they can be overly expensive to install.

Think about photovoltaic panels on the roof, but wait a little longer, the price is very slowly coming down and the products improving. So every year or so get a new price and calculate your potential returns carefully. Keep in mind that fully removing yourself from the grid with these will likely result in the failure of the system before it is paid for, will cost a great deal of money to install, and if you use batteries they will probably fail sooner than you were told. Probably the wisest use of these right now is to slave them to specific appliances like refrigerator freezers, maybe one for your computer. Remember, computers actually require very little energy and if you hire a consultant you can save a lot more by sizing your DC PV system correctly and routing around the computers transformer, or trade the desktop in for a laptop, and get some spare batteries, and a DC direct charger.

Building Codes

In America we have several million people already facing conditions equivalent to the end of the world, we call them homeless people and turn our eyes away. One of the primary reasons these people are required to live on the streets is because we have allowed our government to slowly and incrementally remove our essential rights through the gradual growth of a maze of laws established under the guise of protecting us from ourselves. One of the worst of these is found in the building codes. On one hand building codes are a good thing, as they tend to insure safer places to live, a reasonable expectation that the house you are buying will possess certain consistent qualities, and serve to protect the property values. One the other hand, compliance with the codes has resulted in the requirement for any kind of shelter to meet so many minimum standards that the poor can no longer afford basic shelter. As a result the poor in America are forced into three solutions, no shelter at all, shelter in low income housing subsidized by taxpayers at great expense, and or as is common practice in Los Angeles, often as many as ten families will rent a house designed for one family and cram themselves into a hellish kind of lifestyle in order to realize a solution to their most basic needs.

America needs to address this problem now, and provide policies of government in anticipation, because with the collapse of the fossil fuel society the truly poor will outnumber the basically empowered by a factor of three to one. Think about it, when three quarters of America defaults on their $400,000.00 mortgages what will the governments response be? Will we all be forced out onto the streets because we can't afford fully engineered homes and $25,000.00 worth of government impact fees before we can get a permit to pitch our tents?

In Mendocino County California, a special class was added to the building code, which effectively said a person who owned their own property was allowed to build pretty much whatever they wanted, but they were required to bring it up to code standards or demolish it prior to sale. Sure there are problems that arise, but it is also a fact that building codes have taken away a basic right in private property, if a person owns it's own land, does it really own that land if the government can forbid that person from making improvements to that land, that meet that persons needs? As the wealth of the nation recedes and poverty becomes the normal condition these are questions that will need to be addressed.

Steel Buildings

In recent years steel has become an increasingly popular alternative to wood frame construction in the housing industry, but much of the technology, in part because of excessive building codes has concentrated on systems designed too, as closely as possible, mimic wood frame construction. This condition seriously restricts the potential of steel as an alternative housing medium.

Steel offers several large advantages over wood, the most important of which in this discussion is the ability to design structural and integral weatherproofing skin systems that can be nested, stacked and shipped in remarkably compact packages. Such systems can be incredibly strong, very lightweight, and remarkably inexpensive. When combined with compact isocyanurate foam insulation systems and flexible dry goods for interior finishing a complete very serviceable home can be packaged in a very small container for a very low price.

Such structures can be shipped cheaply all over the planet, hung from steel poles, and used to provide dramatically improved housing as an alternative to the worlds slum developments, with no need for grading. These automatically include intrinsic safety from flooding and mudslides and a host of other advantages. This type of structure needs to be developed and deployed to meet conditions now and in the arriving future, and building codes need to be adjusted appropriately.

An Ideal Storage and Survival Solution

A number of steel building manufacturers currently offer arched and semi arched very inexpensive structures designed primarily for storage and garage style uses.

As the end times begin to arrive more and more people will be seeking an ideal structure in which to store and protect important items needed to enhance their security survivability and sustainability. The ideal solution can be found by updating the example commonly known as the Montana Barn.

One digs a hole three or four feet deep, preferably at an elevated location for drainage, runs a trench with a drain pipe installed that will outflow by gravity to a point lower than the bottom of your hole. The hole should be about a foot bigger than the perimeter of your building. Place a proper perimeter foundation and a proper concrete slab with gravel base and waterproofing membrane below. Then build one of these arched prepackaged steel buildings on your slab.

Make absolutely sure you tell the steel building manufacturer what you are going to do; otherwise your building will most likely collapse. Once your building is up you need to spray the outside with about four to six inches of isocyanurate foam, take special care where the steel structure is attached to the concrete.

Then simply cover the entire structure with the earth you dug out of the hole, try to make sure there is at least six inches of earth covering the very top of the structure, but do not overload it, also you will need to provide a bit of concrete block work and some steps with drainage grate as a single entrance, use a steel door, place a couple of turbo vents in the roof, and you have a building that you can hide in and store important things in and that will survive just about anything nature or man can come up with, and it will cost significantly less than any comparable alternative in function and utility. If you use a little bit of care where you locate it, after a few months of growing in, it can be almost invisible and almost impossible for any casual traveling gangster or miscreant to locate. If you want your storage bunker first class, make it big enough to park a recreational trailer in, run a gravity pipe to a septic system, and feed it from a fresh water tank via gravity on a hill above, with a few solar panels on top and a couple hundred gallons of propane in small tanks, you can survive even a nuclear war with only minor inconvenience.

Chief Nik'e was seated at the big burl wood slab desk that had been installed by his illustrious ancestor in the old Mayor's office at the Commune de Faa'a. Ben was in a nearby chair going through a lap full of mail and tossing the rejects on the polished corral gravel that pretended to be the office floor.

"Lot of bills here Chief, not much money left in the official accounts; here's one from the chief of the Cherokees, United Native American Nations, says he'd like permission to make a state visit next spring for a few weeks."

The great fall of the Howlies had only moderate effects to the lives of the Native Americans, who because of the abuses of the white man had continued a low energy life near the land on their remote reservations. After the fall they unified the tribes under one banner and eventually became a true independent power in what was left of America.

163

International travel for anything other than freight had been rare for two centuries, air travel non-existent, but when people did show up in distant locations, they tended to stay a long time. Chief Nik 'e pondered for a moment.

"I wonder; might be enough folks 'out there' to warrant a return to tourism as a way to find us some of that much needed cash."

Chapter Eleven
Alternate Locations

So what happens if our best efforts come to naught and some or even the worst fears of this book are realized? The best chance for security and survival to the other side of time resides in the co-operative rural community structures we have already discussed. But, as always in real estate, location remains a key factor in success.

We can make use of our model of Arcadia. What was the goal then? 'An idealized garden planet capable of sustaining a significant population essentially forever.' Change the word planet to area, and then look for those areas that might fit that definition already, while keeping in mind all of the conditions that may or are likely to arrive over the next two hundred years. Include in your criteria, factors like probable climate changes, some of these may be positive for certain areas that are marginal now, you can use the climate models published on the Net for this research. But factor in a lot of variables and keep in mind these models are not perfect and cannot anticipate all the arriving conditions perfectly.

There is a probability that much of the Northern areas will suffer significant cooling making them unsuitable for agriculture, so draw some lines on your map. It sounds bizarre as according to the weather models Europe is supposed to suffer the worst cooling, but the line of climactic comfort and survival in Europe is much further north than it is in North America. This is because European climate is not entirely the result of the North Atlantic current but is also heavily influenced by the African Desert and the moderating effects of the Mediterranean. We have a certain proof of this because at the end of the last ice age Cro-Magnon and Neanderthal folks were living right along this line successfully. The line here is roughly along the 45th parallel. In North America it's ten degrees further south more or less along the 35th parallel.

Keep in mind that for a long time during and after the last ice age the Sahara desert was a huge garden area that enjoyed lots of rain, and was covered with lakes and ponds streams and rivers. The same was true of the American desert southwest. This is not to say move to these places now, but does indicate certain places that are very dry in areas north of these regions now, but habitable, may in the not very distant future, that is five to ten years, begin enjoying a wetter more hospitable climate.

However, in North America it is a mistake to take the 35th parallel as the only cold climate avoidance factor because of the Canadian Cold Fronts, which dip more in a wide curve. If there is no major change in climate this line generally runs down the eastern side of Idaho south to take in Montana Wyoming and Nebraska then follows a more or less straight line east northeast towards the bottom of Maine. If you plan on moving north of this line make sure you have the funds and actually purchase a large piece of land with a lot of trees, or coal, or a natural gas well in the backyard, as the winters are already long and brutally cold and will likely only get worse with time. Of course at this juncture the North Atlantic Current might not stop and global warming may proceed with abandon in which case the climates of these areas will likely only improve. At this point in time nobody can predict with authority exactly what will indeed eventually happen so everywhere is something of a gamble.

Despite the hurricanes pounding Florida, and the weird weather all over the place, the scientists continue to tell us there won't be any major climate change for at least a hundred years. That's what we are always told. Nothing bad will happen for at least a hundred years so party on. It's up to you, if you believe them and you don't mind cold weather in the winters, one of the best places in the U.S. to be when the fuel starts to run out is the rural areas of Pennsylvania. Many of those folks have their own natural gas wells in their back yards, piles of lignite down the street, and even a fair amount of oil left in reasonably shallow wells, lots of trees, plenty of rain, not too many people, and for the rest of the planet it's a sort of non-place, so fewer nasty folks will be likely to arrive from the cities. They have lots of rolling hills and good croplands, ponds, barns and readily convertible rural infrastructures in place.

The best security of all can be found on high islands that have a reasonably low population, and good existing self-sufficiency profiles, with a tight nit already near co-operative lifestyle. These continue to exist all over the Mediterranean, and indeed these areas were where true modern civilization began.

There's no way to get around it, you have to have a boat to attack an island, you can't put very many people on a boat so you are always at a disadvantage if you are an attacker, and if you do arrive, the islanders usually have the capacity to absorb your boat population onto the island if you the attacker decide to be peaceful, and there is any room left.

But if you decide to move to any island in the world keep in mind for the short term at least and possibly ultimately, the ocean's sea levels could rise as much as three hundred feet. So you want to locate on an island that has some areas that are at least higher than that. High islands have an additional advantage as they are usually forested, either have game or the potential for game if managed properly, places to hide from invaders, and most importantly, possess running streams and better fresh water resources. These streams not only provide drinking and irrigation water, but are also the most ideal electrical energy resources if or when developed as micro and moderately scaled hydro-electrical resources.

Fish and shellfish surround islands, and climate is moderated by surrounding seas. Greece and Italy are effectively big islands in the Mediterranean and the reasons we have just given are the reasons modern civilization began in these places. Survival was easy enough, so that with a little co-operation folks could greatly reduce the time spent on the basics, then they had time to think about ways to improve their enjoyment of life.

Of course, if you do decide to move to an island, it would be the height of folly to move to one in an area of hurricanes or typhoons, for a while at least these storms are only going to get worse, and moving high and inland offers only a slight degree of protection.

In the U.S. the best areas with all the considerations cranked into the equation, exist in the southern Appalachian and Ozark areas, and in select moderately high areas of the southwest. But these areas will continue to be subject to massive flooding rains, so pick your home and barn location high on a well-drained hill, and think carefully how and where you build. Beware of really high areas like Colorado, while these seem to have game and make you have a sense of security, which can be false, winters are already brutal, and could get a lot worse.

If the South Americans can get past their penchant for procreation and their constant parade of corrupt leaders, they will be able to survive better than any other continent. It may seem perverse to people from the developing world, but those areas currently considered to be poor areas are often considered in that fashion because they have not enjoyed the benefits of a heavily subsidized energy society. As a result, watching the fossil fuels disappear will have only a marginal effect on the way of life they have been living all along. Further many areas in South America continue to possess moderately sized currently undeveloped oil and gas fields.

So in South America you look for areas with the least negative environmental damage, low population and hopefully some kind of infrastructure in place. The U.N. has sponsored these studies and made maps, and the best area in the world, not on an island, likely to survive with minimal impact turns out to be the unlikely nation of Bolivia, followed by the southeastern foothill slopes of the Andes in Peru, and then certain areas of Chili and Argentina.

Most of the population of Bolivia lives in the high Andes, but along the eastern edge, or foothills, there is a vast area of nearly untouched rolling hills, there are few roads, practically no cities, rainfall is and always will be consistent, as in this area the prevailing winds arrive from the vast Amazon rain forests to the east, which also like the Andes serve to insulate whoever lives there from any significant invasion. Here in areas above two thousand feet there are vast regions of rolling forested hills with moderate climate and practically no population, tons of game, ideal country for raising cattle and livestock, lots of fresh water from the Andes, opportunities for hydro electrical power. Etc.

If a well funded group from the developed world were to take a large sum of acquisition and development funds to this area now, they could purchase a few hundred thousand acres and build a community of ranches and farms, that would be able to weather virtually all of the worst possible scenarios the world has to offer, without even a flicker of discomfort. The life of the citizens of this community would be about as good as it gets by any standard in the world right now, they would survive whatever the future has to offer, and come out the other side fully intact and ready to rebuild whatever remained of the planetary society as the new Arcadia, or as whatever they wanted.

But make no mistake, this is not a project anybody should consider alone or if under financed, it would take a lot of money and a lot of work, it is pioneering in the truest sense of the word, and making it work will take a large investment in infrastructure and fully dedicated time, and likely a lot of careful politics. Remember, places like Bolivia, which are desirable in part because they have yet to develop a full fossil fuel energy infrastructure, are often the way they are because of bad political management, and unruly populations. Often these societies already resemble the societies that may arise across the planet in the near term following the fossil fuel collapse. If you move to such a place alone or in a small group, and do a good job, work hard to create a good life, odds are somebody local is going to come and take everything you have created away from you. So places like Bolivia require large numbers of like-minded people, lots of funding, and provisions for military strength. Be careful and plan accordingly.

Also keep in mind that while you may be a highly educated altruistic personality that firmly believes it has risen above the pitfalls of bigotry and racism. In many alternative locations around the world this is not the case, and if you move to such places you may find yourself the victim of reverse racism and resentment by local populations that far outnumber your color and race. These factors will only increase as society heads downhill.

Finally while some of these locations on the list that follows may seem ideal, they are often that way because they have pursued for a long time a policy of very low or zero immigration. Often you must have a very powerful and locally needed skill set combined with a lot of personal monetary assets to even be considered as an immigrant, and sometimes even that will do you no good. Often the only way to relocate to some of the best places is to marry a local citizen.

Here is the list, no place is perfect, no place is immune, but these places will be better off than most.

USA
Kentucky
Tennessee
Arkansas
Parts of Oklahoma
High Country in the Carolina's
Oregon,
Parts of Inland Central and Northern California
Parts of Utah
Hawaiian Islands

If Global Cooling does not arrive:
Southern Washington State and Southern Idaho
Pennsylvania
Ohio
Iowa
Washington State, East of the Cascades

Pacific
New Zealand
Eastern Australia
New Caledonia
Vanuatu

South America
Chile
Argentina
Bolivia
Parts of Peru

Europe
Southern France
Spain
Portugal
Italy, only in the country
Some Greek Islands

In fairness it should be noted that there will be many discrete locations across Asia and Africa, however the Author is totally unfamiliar with these areas, and it is likely that any westerner will stick out like a brightly colored flag in the midst of alien societies and populations, which will for the most part be significantly distressed, so beware. It's also possible that many areas of the middle east will continue to blossom for some time, and while the Author recognizes Islam as the strongest expression of devotion to God on the planet, it is a fact that Islam creates and preserves closed societies in which the white is racially profiled as an infidel, and even if a fully practicing Muslim, rarely accepted, so again beware.

Where is the best place in the world to be? In the Author's opinion it is New Zealand. This area has a good basic infrastructure, will experience little change in its already fine climate, regardless of world climate change, a low population density, a lot of hydroelectric and geo thermal potential that remains untapped, and is effectively based on a still localized agrarian society. But before you pack your bags, know that the New Zealanders are a very intelligent people who know full well the value of what they have and what overpopulation will do to their island, so getting a residence permit in New Zealand is one of the hardest things to accomplish on the planet.

Chapter Twelve
Economic Security Regions

Rural housing co-ops, village co-ops, farm-residential co-ops, the synergistic benefits of anchoring to small rural towns, energy co-ops, all these are discrete small scale structures designed for survival and security in all but the very worst case scenarios, and the best we can hope for even if the worst arrives. As such they are based primarily on the most essential foundation of agriculture and survival off the land.

These structures are small-scale units of last resort, but they also represent alternative social structures that hopefully do not exist alone but as part of a network, these networks can grow to become regions of security because they are based on incremental foundations of basic strength.

Regional Security Zones offer added benefits, greater insulation from insecure areas, large scale co-operation more suitable for grain production and marketing, industrial and manufacturing advantages, until they become equivalent to modern economic security regions.

The purpose of economic security regions in the context of arriving conditions is to decrease the vulnerabilities of large scale economies, so that when those big economies find themselves in retreat, that retreat will slow or stop at the regional levels, thus allowing the maximum possible health of the surviving elements of the economy in times of depression.

For reasons we have already discussed the next depression will in some ways be far worse than the last, but in other ways, it might not be as bad. The secret is that unlike the last depression we have a whole lot of infrastructure and highly productive assets already in place. These assets will not disappear with the economy's collapse. Farms will survive and go on producing food, energy production will go on as it evolves and be transmitted over lines, fuel will be conserved and redirected for use in trucks, trains and tractors, but employment will be localized and travel severely restricted. Money will not disappear but will be worth less than convenient commodities of exchange that possess intrinsic value for barter, while huge quantities of very cheap labor will also be available. That labor will require new basic shelter nearer regional real value enterprises that begin with agriculture, and as a result rural small towns will see significant growth as the cities collapse. The labor pools arriving in these small towns in conjunction with the necessary maintenance of essential transport will present an opportunity for regional essential industry and manufacturing of essential goods and commodities at smaller scales than those currently typical. This is all good as these small to moderate scale industries offer far greater economic security and self sufficiency to discreet regions, and it will be those discreet self sufficient regions which will form the core elements of the surviving human social structure as the world transitions from Fossil Fuel to alternatives and their predicating ways of life.

The strength of each region in terms of energy and economic self-sufficiency along with its distance or insulation from metropolitan areas, will directly determine the level of negative effects it will be forced to endure during the transition, and afterwards. This is true at each social level as we climb the scale, from the single family unit to the co-operatively reengineered small town to the network of self sufficient small towns that form a region then to the network of regions that form a state and then a nation.

The important distinction is that right now industry is primarily in metropolitan areas whose population densities make it effectively impossible for these areas to achieve self-sufficiency. Without huge quantities of energy subsides these places will collapse, while small towns and rural areas will continue and adapt if they can succeed in avoiding being overrun.

Right now our leaders are hell bent on mindless globalization, under the publicly expressed theory that open markets increase manufacturing and extra-national marketing opportunities for our industries, and tend to elevate all of the worlds economic conditions, which in an ideal world tends to make the world a more secure place and improves the lives of all the citizens of the planet. But as we have seen the world is not ideal and without adequate energy, globalization only hastens the use of fossil fuels across the planet, which leads more quickly towards climate change and the negative effects of fossil fuel depletion. We have also seen how globalization primarily benefits the obscenely overpaid heads of major corporations and their major investors at the expense of the productive workers and local economies, and that a large reason globalization is occurring is because these individuals of power and their interests alone, are the actual driving force of world economies.

Further, America has based its economy and its economic decisions on the strength of a ponzi scheme known as the stock market. Almost all of our policies are based on making the artificially inflated value of stocks grow, at the expense of every other sane policy. A stock is supposed to represent a tiny proportionate share of a company's assets and profit margin, but instead those factors have become only a tiny part of the valuation, which like our money is based on an imaginary condition of trust. The value of stock is based on the maximum amount somebody is willing to pay for that stock, not on it's real representational value. Since the number of stocks is limited and demand exceeds supply stocks are artificially inflated and therefore inherently insecure.

Since the perceived value of a company is a projection of its total stock evaluation, the real value of that company is also heavily inflated. So long as trust remains this is healthy to a degree as it provides a way to realize capital for the growth of the company. However this condition of trust is heavily influenced by perception based on quarterly reports of a companies health that are based largely on profit or loss. If a company shows a consistent loss, or even the perception of a future loss the collapse of it's stock value can lead to the collapse of the company, even if that company continues to have real value assets and survivability strengths. This means companies no longer possess primary personal responsibility to their customers or their employees, but instead to the value of their stock.

It is this overriding concern for stock value, in combination with cheap international shipping that has led many American companies to outsource their production foundation to areas of the planet where labor and other production costs are cheaper. As a result America is now a nation of figurehead and management companies who conduct much of their real business in other countries. In the arriving future of fossil fuel depletion this is a dangerous condition.

Right now the idea that America might not have any socks or t-shirts or shoes or pots and pans, or bicycles may seem ludicrous and unimportant, but in the arriving world these things will be critical to our comfort and survival, and they might not be available.

Unions have also played a role in the disintegration of American competitiveness, as have the medical and legal professions, and the overly abusive government regulation and taxation, and even the good-hearted environmentalists. All of these have played their part in increasing the cost of living and working in America to a point where it can find little hope of competing on the world stage.

As a result of all this we should begin to take steps now to grow new institutions from the ground up, restructure our basic business model under the flag of co-operation, in which *all* of the productive members of a company are the ones who benefit from the success of the company, and take responsibility for its failure. This means companies must be restructured one by one, either sanely through perceptive management and reorganization or out of the bankruptcies that are sure to occur as a result of changing social and energy foundation conditions, and as their assets are plundered by their directors and CEO's, and or their shortsighted policies.

Things critical to manufacturing survival in the coming conditions
Alternative energy resources

Oil and fossil fuel costs will be going up around the world more or less consistently in those areas of large population and production capability. Alternative energy sources such as hydro and solar concentrating farms will also go up in terms of cost of product to consumers, and value if owned by independent companies, who will see a dramatic increase in profits. However those same energy alternatives do not escalate *in their cost of production,* so if they are owned by a manufacturing concern, or the manufacturing concern is a participant in an energy co-operative that is based on alternatives, their energy costs will remain constant while competitors' energy costs skyrocket. This means manufacturing will find it beneficial to relocate to areas where alternative energy is available, or create energy alternatives at their manufacturing locations.

In the 1700's and before, industry was located near flowing water, it will be again whenever practical. But now concentrating solar farms will become a big factor and industry relocation to dry deserts will not be a desirable factor, so companies might invest in solar farms, and a structure can be set up in which they receive credit for company owned energy production against actual purchase of locally obtained energy resources.

Reduction in corporate overhead and operating costs

By eliminating overpaid CEO's and sliming non-productive overpaid management staff: No single member of any company can legitimately demonstrate their value to a company is worth $300,000.00 per day. All salaries should be pegged to actual economically provable valuations, and subject to review by democratic process participated in by all tenured members of a company. The rule simply stated is everyone must demonstrate that they produce more value than they consume from the enterprise, if they cannot then their salary should be reduced until it shows equitable justification.

Companies, which are started by, wholly or primarily, owned by individuals, or the result of individually realized technologies should be exempt from this approach. But this does not mean a wealthy individual can be allowed to take over a company and raid it's productivity and viability, therefore sale of a companies' assets regardless of origin should be subject to control by the tenured workforce.

The purpose of this format is simple. If a company increases its costs of doing business through wage increases at any level until it is no longer competitive, in today's world it will be forced into bankruptcy or restructuring through outsourcing, both obviously negative alternatives. The question then is a simple one, is it better to have no job at all, or one in a company that at least insures a reasonable level of existence to all of its contributors.

Reducing medical costs by hiring a company doctor

The current process of generalized health care based on independent doctors who are afraid to make a diagnosis and who seek to maximize their profits from nameless rivers of individuals is broken and destroying America. A large company can find and hire an individual doctor for all it's employees, pay that doctor a good salary for all its general healthcare needs, sign wavers that protect and insulate that doctor from legal issues, and instead employ the old and proven method of firing for incompetence. The doctor can then safely make diagnosis's, reduce or eliminate its medical malpractice insurance and deal with the majority of the medical issues of its clientele base directly.

Companies will save millions of wasted dollars, hospitals will be forced to streamline costs and abusive layers will have to find other ways to screw the public.

Obviously HMO's are the alternative here, but HMO's are also for profit mega corporations that thrive by forcing out local competition. These fall under the heading of nationally critical services and as such need to be reorganized as not for profits which are enhanced by government protection from fraudulent and excessive mal-practice lawsuits.

Eliminate unions who constantly push for higher wages until the company is bankrupted by those wages

No worker should be paid ten times more than the value of its productivity in the company, in co-operatively owned companies unions are a liability that can simply be discarded, because the company is the union.

For the purposes of this discussion economic security regions may be defined as those areas or regions that can support a variety of socially critical enterprises without the necessity of export. For instance, a company that makes shoes should be able to survive in a reasonably local region, by making the shoes necessary for its local population and thus providing a justification for its own existence as well as providing a critical product for the people of its supporting region. This is important for several related reasons.

1. Small to moderately scaled manufacturing provides economic resources for localized economies, increases general wealth and stability for local economies, and provides alternatives to agricultural jobs. These factors help to insure regional stability.

2. As the fossil fuel resource begins its cycle down, the cost of exporting and shipping long distances will increase dramatically. This means the cost of a pair of shoes made in China even if the cost at the factory is far below the local cost will increase until they are no longer able to compete with the local manufacturer. But people will still need shoes.

3. In a fossil fuel based economy it makes sense to have one huge factory located near the largest and cheapest possible labor pool, in a post fossil fuel economy it no longer makes sense and important brands will need to consider the viability of decentralization, downsizing and modularization or

franchising of facilities. To be clear, large metropolitan areas will no longer be viable when the fuel shortages arrive, long distance shipping will no longer be viable when the fuel shortages arrive, if social structures are to survive at any significant level manufacturing needs to become decentralized and regional in nature.

Ben was going over the annual budget for next year.

"Looks like we're going to be short of funds again Chief?" Nik'e had a pained look on his face.

"You're right Ben, hate to admit it, but I guess it's time for another trip out to Noa Ville... You want to come along?"

"Can I bring Taea?"

"Sure, might be a good idea to bring some boots as well, my old bones are telling me it might be a good idea to hike the trail up to the Marae on Mount Oropiro. I could use your loud voice to yell at Oscar, in Rohutu Noa Noa, he solved the population problem on Tai'iti once maybe he has some answers now."

Chapter Thirteen
Investing for Security
and the New World

In an inflationary economic environment arriving from shortages of foundational commodities the primary investments that will continue to increase in *real* value are foundational commodities. This includes types of real estate we have discussed that offer the potential for security and a reasonable way of life.

Keep in mind that the world economy is based on paper, and that paper is based on nothing at all but an imaginary condition of public trust. You can't eat it, you can' t drink it, you could burn it but not for very long. It's a medium only, with zero intrinsic real value. So for convenience and imagined greater security you might consider investing in gold, but even though gold is rare, it has little useful or real intrinsic value.

The first order of priority is to use some of your funds to acquire your retreat. If you have enough you should pay cash for your retreat, or make sure you have the funds to pay off your notes, should the need arrive. Do not count on the value of your city home to accomplish this, as that value will dramatically depreciate well before the real need to relocate arrives.

The second priority, if you want to increase your personal level of security and lifestyle enjoyment is to either stock your basement, or build a highly secure survivable alternative structure, (perhaps like the one suggested in chapter 7 under 'Architecture-Steel buildings') and stock it with important essential commodities that possess a long storage life, and with essential tools.

If you decide that social continuity is indeed going to fail, you should consider three commodities in particular, tobacco, distilled liquor, and instant coffee. Even if you don't smoke, drink, or even if you are a tea drinker. These products will become the high value concentrated mediums of exchange, and inherently possess very long shelf lives. Follow these with medical supplies and multiple vitamins. Next comes fuel. But take care to protect your storage from fire, weather, and the disintegration of the container.

Consider coal; right now in states like California coal is almost universally forbidden as a home heating or cooking fuel, and so is hard to find. However, coal can be stored outside uncovered, and will last forever, it is very concentrated energy, and can be converted to diesel and gas. If our leaders had foresight we would be locating huge stockpiles of coal at centralized locations across the country right now, to serve the same purpose as the strategic oil reserves. A person that has frozen to death for lack of heat in the winter is not terribly concerned with the quality of the air. To many Americans right now this may sound ludicrous, but if the economy collapses or even continues on its current path the number of people freezing to death in their homes in the winter is going to accelerate altogether too quickly.

Even if your retreat has ten acres of trees, those trees are going to get used up faster than you can grow new ones, a good supply of coal can make a huge difference in this situation. Right now coal is cheap, and will be an excellent commodity for trade in the arriving future conditions. So even if you have no plans on burning any of it right now it's a good idea to buy a good stock to hold in storage.

Also keep in mind that if you are freezing, and cutting down live trees to keep warm, a few bags of coal are equal to a good sized live tree. That tree will go on absorbing CO_2 and making clean air for a very long time, and is likely worth a great deal more to the environment than the damage you cause by burning an equivalent amount of coal. But if you do burn coal use it sparingly it can burn really hot, and it is dirty, so make sure to clean your chimney frequently or you will get a chimney fire much sooner than expected and likely burn down your house.

Food is difficult, most canned goods have a shelf life of about four or five years at most, even carefully and expensively packaged survival rations, begin to deteriorate at seven years. So the best you can do is invest a little in these and then wait until you see conditions are definitely going to get serious, then load up.

Alternatively, consider the wisdom at the beginning of this part, if you buy a container of instant coffee at the first sign of the beginning of the oil powered inflationary spiral for $8.00 it is likely that same jar will cost $15 or even $20 a couple of years later, while the same investment in the stock market will be worth about ten cents. The same thing applies to all basic long shelf life commodities. Just don't forget to include the cost of your storage building in your calculations.

An important tool set that can dramatically increase food storage life includes vacuum plastic bag sealing machines, these come in scales for small convenient food storage, and larger heavier sizes and weights commonly sold for packaging and decreasing the storage size requirements of bedding and cloths. Poke a hole in a sack of dry pinto beans, stick in an old sock with some moisture absorbing chemicals, stick the lot in one of those plastic bags, and suck out all the air and seal. Kept in a cool dry place your beans will last for twenty years, so long as the rats and mice are kept away.

When you are buying your retreat, think carefully about a good location for planting a food garden, and make sure you can arrange some kind of irrigation that does not require deep pumping from a well or reliance on commercial water that requires lots of electricity to get to your house. Right now cheap oil means the food we buy is cheap because it is created in the equivalent of factories that run on huge amounts of fossil fuels at each stage of production, so it's usually cheaper to work at a wage scale job and buy food from the market than it is to spend the time needed to grow and process it for storage. This situation will change dramatically over the next few years.

Right now agriculture in America requires the equivalent of over 400 gallons of oil to feed each American each year, and while as things worsen it is likely that priority fuel use will be granted to agriculture, it is also true that the cost of food will rise dramatically and quickly. This situation will only grow worse, as agriculture will reduce the use of pesticides, soil amendments and irrigation, which will cause cropland destruction and loss of productivity as time progresses, even as the inertia of population growth continues to increase demand. Ultimately loss of the fossil fuel subsidy may in fact lead to a near total collapse of the American agricultural industry. It may be hard for many American's to even imagine, but it is a fact that actual pervasive starvation in America is a real possibility in the not very distant future.

So, it is a good bet you will be growing your own food or starving. You will need to invest in fencing and in America you will likely be eating a lot of potatoes as your basic homegrown staple. A good rule of thumb is that it will require about 1/5ᵗʰ to ¼ acre of land in potatoes alone for each person, and it just goes up from there. Remember the village figures once again, sustainability requires about four or five acres per family of four per year, and by now it is likely a co-operative village is looking a lot less radical as an option than it did initially.

Again, get the Permaculture Books and the French Biodynamic books and plan your gardens accordingly as best you can because it is a near certainty that your ultimate survival depends on the productivity of your own gardens in the surprisingly near future.

If your gardens, rabbit hutches, and chickens are installed and producing you will need to get stuff to preserve and store your yields. Once again, wood stoves, smokers for meat preservation, jars for canning and on and on. Yes all of this is a huge hassle and a huge investment, but if you want to understand the importance of this in a visceral way, next weekend, stop eating for two days, and while you are fasting, fully imagine that steak you have set aside as your reward at the end of your fast will not be there at all in the coming world. Unless you prepare you *will* eventually starve, and a person who has food in that un-brave new world will find little value in your fist full of paper dollars.

Avoid *reliance* on freezers, even solar powered freezers may breakdown, and the means to fix them might not exist. However, if it is likely you will have long term electricity by all means get a high efficiency refrigerator freezer, and a few critical spare parts. Probably forty to fifty percent of the $1,000 refrigerator freezers in the U.S. are thrown away because of the failure of either a five dollar solenoid switch that often fails from power surges, and or the failure of a ten dollar freezer fan, both parts can be replaced in less than half an hour by any even remotely handy person if you have the parts on hand. So obviously, it pays to buy the spares in advance.

A healthy supply of tools is critical. Especially basic hand tools for gardening, digging, and firewood procurement and processing. Chainsaws will be critically important. Make sure you have at least two of the same model, as this will allow you to steal parts from the one that breaks to keep the other one working. Keep a very good supply of fuel for these in carefully sealed and protected containers.

Rifles: If only one, chose a 22 long rifle that can use bird shot, as this will supply you with the widest possible variety of game, with the most commonly available ammunitions. For personal defense a pump action, straight barrel 12 gauge shotgun, but make sure you check the action carefully, as some of these in attempting to be overly safe are very difficult to operate. Make sure it will take the full variety of shells, and be careful to get a good supply of the right sized ammunition for the particular model.

If you are going to be in a major wilderness situation, and might be shooting big game from a long distance, a quality 22 magnum with a good scope is probably more than adequate.

If you are going to get serious and buy pistols, think about a quality long barrel unit with a scope that can double as an effective lightweight hunting alternative, avoid macho and city guns, and be legal. Keep your hardware simple, fancy semi automatic assault weapons and even complex supposed survival rifles can breakdown and may require exotic ammunition that will be hard to find. It is also always better to avoid confrontation.

Do not discount the value of a good compound bow and a good supply of arrows. These are silent, and a good hunter can be very effective for a very long time with one of these, and, with a small amount of applied skill you can never run out of ammo.

Avoid diesel and gas generators, they consume huge amounts of fuel over time and will breakdown permanently within a relatively short time period. If you can't install a micro hydro system, and you can afford it, you can at least have some electricity in the day with solar panels. Even small ones can be utilized to run laptop computers, which can allow you to plug into the Internet during the day. This will be an important tool for finding out what is going on in the world as things power down. Also keep in mind that if you do manage to secure a good self sufficient electrical source, if you burn your lights at night in the new world environment, this will act like a bright beacon that will draw undesirables to your home, so use care.

Get oil lamps, the simpler the better, and think about what is important to you in living out your life on a long term basis, then try to figure out and find alternatives that are simple, do not require electricity, and for which you might be able to improvise alternative sources of energy if you were forced too.

Remember, in the 1700's and early 1800's people were still able to live good reasonably comfortable civilized lives. Study how they lived and what they used and apply what you learn to your own situation.

Once you've got your retreat in order, and your supplies well stocked, if you still have monies left over, you may need to find more abstract investments.

Again commodities are key market style investments, but pursue this type of investment only if you are willing to spend a lot of energy learning the rules of the game very carefully, and then willing to keep a close eye on all the complex variables that are always constantly changing. Oil stocks and futures might be a good candidate, but keep in mind; these companies and their assets will be the first candidates for nationalization when things start to go bad.

If you desire to be a good Arcadian consider investing in alternative energy. Invest in your local Energy CO-OP first, if one doesn't exist spend some energy to see about sitting one up, but try to make sure it's based at least partly on some kind of local renewable assets and technologies.

Next invest in major alternative energy projects; especially major scale solar farms that use proven technology. You have to be careful in the overall alternative energy field, it's full of new and arriving technologies and many of these will be either fraudulent or honestly result in non-viability as their development evolves. Wind farms are an example, wind technology is currently often subject to serious and expensive maintenance and breakdown problems, especially about the time their government subsides evaporate, so if you chose this venue look to proven reliability over high output or technically sophisticated units. Remember, this field, like all energy fields is hugely benefited by economies of scale, it is usually better to join with others and get a bigger unit near large scale infrastructure farms than it is to try this on your own. Avoid complex technologies no matter how appealing, things like fuel cells are expensive, may have short lifetimes and usually require processed fossil fuels.

It is very important to two make several points clear.

1. Despite the cautions. If we fail to invest in energy alternatives now and in a very big way, we will collapse in the not too distant future, first economically and then socially across almost the entire planet. Remember, the basic definition of bankruptcy is the inability to pay your debts on time. America has been unable to pay its debts on time with real monies, for a very long time and has been making up imaginary monies. It calls these imaginary monies borrowing against trust. All or most of the world's economies are now based entirely on a condition of trust in the future, and without adequate energy, there is no future. As a result the moment the condition of trust in the future fails, all of the world's economies become subject to collapse. Adequate energy is absolutely critical to the survival of modern economies and societies.

2. The term, 'Energy alternatives' is not limited by so called 'green' energies, it includes alternative ways to harvest any kind of fossil fuel, nuclear, and potentially others. Green Energy alternatives will always be

better, but at this juncture, because we are so late in the game, it is absolutely critical that we insure adequate energy regardless of origin because without it there will be a collapse, there will be no resources available to recover from the collapse, and no hope of installing adequate long term green energy alternatives, and therefore, no hope of permanently fixing the environmental problems we have created by burning fossil fuels.

3. If you think the nuclear disposal problem is difficult to deal with and dangerous now, consider how much more dangerous it will be when the world finds itself in a state of total economic and social collapse. The rotting open tanks of spent fuel will not be taken care of, the mega reactors will not be properly decommissioned, none of the waste will be protected deep underground in Nevada. The new generation of pellet reactors can help solve these problems by providing time and money to accomplish at least the less damaging solutions to our past mistakes. It's also important to note that nuclear does not contribute to the greenhouse gas problem.

4. Invest in localized energy Co-ops based on alternatives, especially hydro. Remember, unless you are a huge mega corporation or a nation, hydro power does not require a major damn. Small and moderately scaled hydro facilities can now be located wherever there is naturally occurring running water, even along coastlines in the ocean. If you are in an agricultural or rural area look into gasification systems, particularly those that can be adapted to make transportable fuels other than electricity.

5. Invest in companies that produce products, which either operate with reduced energy requirements or conserve energy. Remember, our energy supply will not disappear over-night, the fear resides in the energy inflationary spiral. This means as energy begins to cost more any product that requires less to do an equivalent job, will cost less to operate and therefore will be cheaper and more competitive, therefore its company will be more successful. Obviously this means vehicles, gas appliances, wood stoves, and so on, but keep in mind that a vehicle manufacturer that stubbornly continues to make gas guzzling vehicles along with gas conserving hybrids will have to offset its gains from energy conservation products with it's losses from energy abusive products.

Look into local agricultural corporations. Farming is now a large scale enterprise, and because food will always be a national and basic priority, if any civilization is left at all, resources will be directed to farms for food production. That food will be extremely valuable, and the most efficient possible methods will continue to be employed until the very end. This means large-scale farms will remain. In some cases these will become so expensive to develop and maintain that agricultural corporations will arrive as an alternative financing vehicle. If you do your homework, you can in effect become a gentleman farmer by simply investing in these shares. The shares will not only give you a good return in most cases, but also likely entitle you to a priority share of the actual produce. Owning constantly renewing produce in the arriving times will be a very important asset.

But again be careful, at the time this book is being written agriculture in America is very risky and subject to a very low margin of profit. This is because, numerous nations across the planet especially segments of the developing world are not subject to the costs and controls our government and economy places on American farmers, and because right now shipping is cheap. This condition will be changing over the next few years, so if you invest now do not look for major profits immediately, instead be prepared to hang in for a few years. Also take care to make an informed decision based on potentially changing climate factors. Keep in mind that even our finest state of the art systems still cannot predict what will happen with absolute authority, so you just have to do the best you can.

Likewise look to big industrial and processing agriculture related companies for likely reliable long-term stock investments.

Again, invest in your local, hopefully rural community, that's largely what the whole thing is all about. A community of friends is better in all ways than a solitary existence. There is however one very important difference between then and now. As an American you have been taught, however discretely that your role is to get as much from the other guy as you can while giving back as little as possible. In the small community of the arriving future this kind of conduct will quickly get you excommunicated. If anybody is going to survive all of us will have to get past that philosophy and learn to give as much as we can and work together towards common goals, if we can't do that we are all well and truly screwed. So your best investment of all is to invest in your fellow humans and the environment we all share.

Of course Nik'e wasn't expecting to talk to the ancient soul of Chief Oscar, he wasn't even absolutely sure there was an afterlife, or a real place called Rohutu Noa Noa, that's partly why he felt obligated to try as hard as he did to insure the best facsimile of Noa Noa here on the islands in this life. But there was that solar powered laptop hidden in the Marae on top of the mountain, with all the wisdom of the ancients on its hard drive. Why Chief Oscar had to put it way up there he had no idea, and he grumbled to himself about the long walk up the mountain. But he had to admit, in a very real way that laptop meant he would be able to listen to the now ancient wisdom of his ancestor, and maybe, just maybe find a solution or two to the current problems he faced.

Chapter Fourteen
Religion and Affirmations

Is there an Arcadian religion, what is it? Maybe; perhaps eventually; whatever it is it will include the reality that DNA evolution is real, that we are as earthlings, the result of the DNA's activities here over four billion years, and that our star allows those activities to continue for possibly four billion more years; that we have achieved a state of majority and are therefore personally and globally responsible for our activities, within the envelope that the functions of life have created for us; that the natural world of life, all of it, is a truly ancient miraculous marvelous, glorious and even hallowed thing.

Does this entail nature worship? In a regimented doctrinal sense no, but in a deeper mystical sense maybe it does. Evolution as an aspect of religion is the most ancient of all possible affirmations of the human experience on the Earth. It's a fact that it is the physical structure of all life; it's a fact that it has been working away on this planet alone for Four Billion years. It's likely it is not unique to this place, but exists across the entire universe in rare but blessed places, that it began at or near the birth of the entire universe, and likely is an enveloping technology of the true original mind of creation.

If you stand in a forest quiet and alone, it can become almost difficult to fail to hear the mystical antiquity of life speaking directly to your soul, and know that soul is in the midst of its ancient home. Sure there is always a hint of fear insecurity, maybe guilt and humility, but isn't that what we're supposed to feel when we stand in the presence of God.

Is the Earth to be taken as Gaia the earth mother in a literal God like sense? A person's religion should always be the direct result of a person's personal growth, not something somebody else demands as a result of power or even simple inertia. The Earth was a dead place before DNA and the life it sponsored showed up, and there can be no question, even in a purely secular interpretation, that the comprehensive expression of life, as both the true essence and the sum of Gaia's mystical and physical presence *represents* a living entity of great import, and there is no question that we owe that system for the experience of our life here; even as a purely secular vehicle this affirmation is a healthy thing. But is GAIA a living singular synergistic entity worthy of worship? If the earth is a living entity, it has been alive for four billion years and will likely live four billion more, to that kind of entity your needs are less important than the needs of a single ant are to you, so you would most likely be better off to pray to a rock. Nevertheless techniques that lead to total immersion within the consciousness of this being do exist and are practiced by certain mystical religions. The full realization of this state can be one of the most powerful mystical experiences available to the human condition, and can lead to the ability to perform certain levels of magic, like calling the wind, calming the storm, making it rain and so on.

Is there an entity like The Greater God or Great Spirit, The Author believes there is, that the universe has a vast mystical aspect; that there are untold forms of experience and being, and numerous hierarchies within the varied realities implied, all as a result of direct personal experience. He finds absolutely no conflict or detriment in his belief system with the fact of DNA evolution. However, it is very clear that, at least for the time being, whatever greater beings there might be, they are not immediately involved in directing the path of our lives or our futures. For better or worse, that seems to be entirely up to us, because again for better or worse in a very real sense we have graduated to become the immediate Gods of our own small dominion.

Is that blasphemy? Being God is sort of like being president of a nation, in the Authors opinion it is not a job anybody in his or her right mind would want. So maybe the universe is full of greater beings but none of them are dumb enough to take that role, so the role always stays open and greater beings just show up now and then as teachers, usually disguised as normal local folks, to help the natives along a bit. The really big guys like to play with really big creations, but are wise enough to turn them loose to evolve on their own. Who Knows?

Hunter Yeats in his book 'Being' said it best. 'There are certain principles, abstractions and conditions of thought, ultimate truths that transcend all possible levels of being.' Both Good and Evil are always necessary aspects of any dynamic reality that supports perceptive experience; their alternate names are constructive and destructive. Real growth will always arrive out of the constructive, but the destructive will always be more enticing and the easier path to follow. Betrayal in all of its forms will always be the essential verb of evil. The driving ethic of effective and constructive growth at our level of being is Responsible Altruistic Self Interest.'

The driving goal of the Arcadian concept is nothing short of the complete terraforming evolution of the human condition on the Earth in real, constructive, and grounded ways, always towards an evolving Utopian vision that makes a basic assumption. The Earth and the Human condition can always be better than it is.

What example can we look towards as an ideal model for being human, the Author believes the greatest concentration of such beings resides currently in the native populations of Islands of Polynesia. It is a certainty they are not all perfect, but taken as a whole they could be described as an enlightened nation of Bodhisattvas, who have failed to realize what they are. Highly educated at once both simple and deeply complex folks who just enjoy living life close to nature, in peace with their fellows, in the midst of paradise.

Before the French and English showed up and did their best to mess up paradise, the dominant Polynesian Religion was known as Arioi, pronounced Ah-Roy. The adherents of Arioi would have been right at home in the ancient Arcadian Realm once ruled by the Great God Pan. They believed in sex, and lots of it, without restraint, but never without the full consent and participation of the partners. To an Arioi both sexes were absolutely equal halves of a constantly evolving being.

The Arioi could in fact have been taken straight out of the pages of a Tom Robbins comedy, as on a superficial level they were an exact cross between a traveling version of 'Another Roadside Attraction, and the Bandaloop Dancers, worshipers that would have made The Great God Pan dance with joy. Nobody ever said religion had to be stuffy burdensome and depressing. In the old days the extensive 'priesthood' of the Arioi were composed of traveling theatre groups that presented comedy acts and plays for the general entertainment of the islanders. In the process they also acted as the inter-island newscasters, and as important serious advisers to the tribal chiefs.

They were always festooned with flowers and feathers, and were into tattoos in a big way. You had to earn your tattoos so they were a sign of accomplishment. A novice or common neophyte was entitled only to a ankle band, and then it went on in stages until you got to a grand master, who was literally covered head to toe with works of art, So in all ways the Arioi were literally and figuratively a colorful lot. Perhaps their most powerful public ceremony was the practice of fire walking often accompanied by a powerful and mesmerizing native drum band.

Recently there has been a small rebirth of the Arioi in Polynesia, much to the consternation of the 'decent' Polynesian folk that abound on the islands, as well as the French. The Arioi believed in small deities of the forest and areas of the sea, a great God of the Sea, and One of the Land, and a great God Oro who presided over all Creation. They believed in a mystical level of the spirit, life after death and a heavenly realm called Rohutu Noa Noa, or The Fragrant Paradise, which was immediate as it could almost be touched with the fingers from the tops of certain high mountains.

Perhaps most importantly Arioi religion was distinguished by priests whose primary job was to listen with a careful ear to natural conditions around them, and by a primary ethic that included personal responsibility. Unlike the concept of sin, the failure of personal responsibility to an Arioi did not necessarily mean the loss of enjoyment in the afterlife, but instead included immediate punishment by local gods, in this life, and importantly the possibility of punishment by fellow villagers and chiefs.

Acceptable personal responsibility was defined by a constantly evolving set of forbiddens known as Tapu's, which the reader will likely recognize in it's western translation as Taboo's.

Tapu's were emplaced by priests and at priest's requests by village chiefs and resulted in effect in the Polynesian version of a system of laws. One class of tapu's were primarily concerned with social and spiritual conduct and changed only slightly over time, but the second class was more fluid and was primarily concerned with the preservation of the surrounding environment and the food resources the environment provided. Arioi priests were charged with the role of environmentalists and naturalists, they listened too and carefully observed the effects of population and over harvesting of resources, and when these things became damaging declared Tapu's, which gave the subject resources, time to recover.

Westerner's have a tendency to look down on the belief systems of others, and to force their point of view wherever they go. This unfortunate attitude has resulted in innumerable wars, which continue to this day. While Arioi sexual practices and proclivities may be a little excessive in today's social climate, every other aspect of Arioi is entirely appropriate as a healthy structure of belief especially in the arriving conditions. It's also a fact that almost alone among the worlds races, the Polynesians have managed to offend practically no one else. Like all religions Arioi has a superficial level, and a far deeper and more sophisticated mystical level, which will be recognized by the more mystical and deeper participants of any of the worlds religions as very close to the universal truth.

As a result of all these factors, Arioi might serve as the foundational basis for a new and resurrected modern world religion, a religion easily capable of automatically absorbing the positive aspects of all the other world religions and mysticisms in a truly egalitarian manner. Responsible adaptation of the Arioi religion by persons who decide to follow the Arcadian set of philosophies would result in a universal religious and social structure that would offend few, would automatically improve world social conduct, and provide a basis for evolution of the human spirit in a healthy personally responsible manner long into the future. Of course overtly promiscuous sex, and tattoos would hopefully remain at the discretion of the adherent and not the priests.

Chapter Fifteen
Pillars of Wisdom

According to the Human DNA record, we arrived as the human species on the earth as a result of the mutation of a single gene and the birth of a single then odd and curious child about 230,000 years ago, probably in South Africa. That child was successful and multiplied its gene, until there was a large nation of millions of hunter gathers spread across most of the planet. Then about 75,000 years ago something happened, most likely a super volcano exploding in The South East Asian Sea. This event caused a global climate change event that suddenly shrunk the world's human population down to just about fifteen thousand people. Imagine that, fifteen thousand souls had the whole planet all to themselves.

It took them all that time to get to the overpopulated mess we find ourselves in now. If the worst combinations of the possible negative futures we have discussed come to pass, it won't require a super volcano or an asteroid to get us back to a state of affairs closely resembling the world those fifteen thousand enjoyed. Since the odds are unfortunately pretty strong that something like this could happen in the not too distant future, it seems like a good legacy to initiate a project that would make it as easy and quick as possible for the folks that are left to recover some of the better aspects of modern society. The best way to do this seems to be to plant records of our best, and perhaps worst accomplishments at a wide variety of locations likely to survive and be desirable places to live, in whatever is left of the future planet.

We can assume that some of the folks will still remember some form of English, but it also seems appropriate to employ regional major language streams as well.

If they are going to have an impact they need to be located in places of stable conditions and at locations of some type off intrinsic attractability, and they need to be placed into some kind of very protective structures that are not too difficult to access, but at the same time, not likely to be trashed by transient idiots. So some kind of almost religious seriousness needs to be incorporated into these monuments in some way, and if they are going to be successful there needs to be a lot of them.

Books are low tech, but are usually self destructive, mildew, rats, acid in the paper, and very bulky, while computer style media is high tech, requires electricity and might not work, but is compact and so efficient that we could put whole encyclopedias and probably most of the script in the library of congress on a single laptop. Right now the idea that the world's libraries might disappear may seem a little ludicrous, but keep in mind that to a freezing or starving person a book is a really handy bit of fuel. More than one end of the world film has put that little group of sorry survivors around a smoky campfire on the floor of the public library.

So, this is a good project for somebody to think about seriously. In the Author's opinion we might try locating small steep weather proof pyramids made of concrete or stone or wrapped in stainless steel, with some kind of inscription on the outside. Something like 'There is a treasure inside, but unless you are King Arthur and know the secret, if you mess with this place you will die' maybe a skull symbol to scare off folks who can't read and therefore will be of little value if they find the library. Put them in all the national parks of the world in central locations that are easily accessible and have some kind of universal appeal.

Inside, a specially engineered laptop with a touch activated screen, and various simple symbols that activate various programs automatically. With it you put a library of DVD's used for information storage, (no funky jewel cases to take up space) to back up the hard drive, and a small photovoltaic panel. The laptop has to work with the solar panel alone, even if the batteries are long since dead, but if we were to include spare lithium ion batteries in sealed containers it wouldn't hurt. In it you put encyclopedias, books about how things work, great works of literature, histories that include how we screwed up, plans for both simple and complex technologies of usefulness.

Is this the ultimate best solution to this issue, probably not. Does it seem corny right now? Sure. But the probabilities are very high that for somebody finding one of these units two or there hundred years in the future it could be the single most important event in their history of mankind on the earth. On the other hand if everything works out for us in fairy tail manner, it remains likely, the threat of near extinction will always remain at some level to all human societies that may arise. In that event every few hundred years they could open the crypts and replace the system with new and improved technologies, then the academics and historians of their day would be able to enjoy dissecting the quaint contents with their students, while wondering at the strange experience of being human on the earth.

Remember it is a *fact* that the fossil fuels are running out and will in the not very distant future cease to exist completely. Think about that world, no coal no oil no gas at all, nowhere. Children that are born today may live to see that world. Even if Armageddon arrives and a few people survive and start rebuilding the world, they will not be able to restart the industrial revolution, ever, for four billion years.

We are condemning all the people that might follow us to live out their experience of life here in bark huts eating acorn mush. If you are a Howlie Indian lover you might think this has a certain romantic appeal from your easy chair, as you watch "Dances with Wolves". My ancestors lived this life, and my backyard has an ancient camp around a small cave in a mound of big rocks, I think about it all the time, it most certainly is *not* the best we can be.

This is our last few moments of opportunity to develop the alternatives, because we can't develop the sophisticated technologies needed for the alternatives without oil and the world infrastructure that oil has granted us. If we don't do this and there is a future for mankind on this planet we will certainly be remembered as the most evil generation of man ever to exist, because we squandered the opportunities for all the possible futures. Think about that when you're ripping up the national forests in your Hummer or your ATV, or burning up a hundred gallons an hour in your yacht.

It is my personal hope that if anybody actually steps up and performs this project, that they will include very clear instructions on how to make beer, grow grapes and make wine, plans for a still and a picture of an oak tree and a barrel wouldn't hurt either.

Noah's first activity after he got off the ark was to plant grapes. He knew God personally, he also knew life really wasn't worth living, if you weren't allowed to enjoy yourself at least some of the time. It's up to us and nobody else to insure that at least for a little bit of each life lived in the 80,000,000 generations of humanity that may follow here, a little bit of enjoyment is allowed.

Afterward
Noa Ville 2300

Yazuli Nik'e, Ben and Taea were on a boat, actually more of a ship, the once sleek, now suffering super yacht 'Oro', that served as one of the primary inter-island ferries. Oro was a 120' sailing catamaran built in France near the turn of the 21st century, in nautical terms any boat that survives intact for a century is almost miraculous, The Oro was now well over two hundred and even though she had been lovingly restored many times over, was definitely showing her age. Nevertheless, because of her huge deck area and quick sailing ability she remained ideal as an island ferry and the Polynesians were loath to give her up.

Nik'e and Ben were in the pilot house lounge trying their best not to spill their coffee, Taea was out on the forward 'beach' enjoying the ride, as the Oro approached Passé Nao Nao the southern pass through the reef into the lagoon that surrounded the sister islands of Raiatea-Tahaa.

In the old days Uturoa had been the capital town of these two blessed islands, and it remained a bustling little center of commerce, but during the time of the Howlie downfall when all the mega yachts and their wealthy owners had more or less intentionally stranded themselves in the Societies, an astute guest on one of those yachts had been bumming about the islands and realized the area around the Baie Faatemu at the southern end of Raiatea was just about the finest location on the entire planet to develop a secure self sufficient community that could last effectively forever.

So a few of the superrich got together and ordered a huge shipment of supplies and materials from the states, filled up two freighters at great expense, it turned out to be one of the last transpacific oil powered shipments.

Then they developed the village and environs that would come to be known as Noa Ville. It was an appropriate name as many still believed the old Arioi legend that Rohutu Noa Noa, the fragrant paradise of the afterlife, could actually be touched by an upraised arm from the summit of the adjacent Mount Oropiro, of course the allusion to Noah of the Ark seemed appropriate as well, Now there was a busting small town and harbor around the mouth of the river, and a population of about three thousand lucky souls who had gone on living the richest of lives while the world collapsed around them, a golf course and extensive parks and large damn high up in the valley above that provided all the electrical needs, terraced fields and plots of Taro. So Noa Ville was where most of the big money in the Societies ended up, and Yazuli Nik'e was here on yet another begging mission, looking for funds and possible solutions to the overpopulation issues now once again troubling Tai'iti Nui.

"No Ben, the old world didn't collapse because there wasn't enough oil to go around, it collapsed because there were too many people using too much of everything and too few willing to part with any of their luxuries. It collapsed when the demand for energy permanently exceeded the world's ability to produce enough of it. That caused an inflationary spiral, which caused an economic collapse, and because all the worlds great economies were by then inextricably tied together the whole thing really collapsed and when it did the conditions this false economy had created that allowed so many people to survive also collapsed, so that between the energy shortages and the economic collapse it created, people started to starve all over the place, and the starving people tore the whole thing down in a great riot that lasted for three years. Then, some people said it was terrorists that stole it from a Russian lab, some said it was too sophisticated and had to come from America, all we know for sure is somebody turned the flox loose and in one horrendous year over four billion people died.

There is a debate that goes on to this day, if the Flox hadn't been released just about the entire world would most likely have ended up back in the stone ages, so in effect it was the Flox that saved the planet, on the other hand the intentional murder of four billion people has to be the greatest evil any one can imagine, and to our ancestors that lived through it in the rest of the world it was the greatest evil of all time. But strong pockets of society survived, and suddenly there were plenty of resources to go around. It's taken all this time to put things back together again but now the world seems to be coming together in a newly blossoming age of reason. So in effect the world was saved by the greatest possible act of evil. The Arioi priests love to sit around and argue about that one.

Most of the people that survived were holed up in remote locations like us, and for fifty years after that everybody was afraid to travel or let anybody from outside in, so the whole world fragmented and then slowly stabilized. The only real threat left was from the nuclear aircraft carriers and their battle groups, but fortunately for us they ended up protecting the oil resources, the refineries and the convoys, from pirates.

At the time of the collapse there were almost twice as many people on Tai'iti, and except for a couple of really small turbines, and the big dam in the middle, all the island's power came from an oil fired plant. We survived well, because Oscar Great chief installed bigger turbines on almost all the rivers, and moved most of us back out to the outer islands. He also put those big wind turbines in, which in his old age turned out to be one of his biggest regrets, but the big gasifier was also his idea, run our cars and kitchens on gas from garbage. Everybody thought he was out of his mind, I've even heard he had his own doubts, and the damn thing was a pain until all the kinks got worked out, but where would we have been all these years without it. Then he got the Arioi's in gear, and they got people running around all over the place planting fruit trees, and hatching chickens like mad and let his friend Jean sit up the big fish hatchery and put in the gene splicing lab at the Botanical gardens, and hey we even had big juicy tomatoes in Tai'iti while the rest of the world fell into hell.

But now the population's started becoming a problem again, and we can't go back to the old Arioi solution, so the only thing I've been able to think of is trying to get New Caledonia New Zealand and Hawaii to take some of our people.

So far I haven't had much luck, but the ambassador in Hawaii made an interesting suggestion, he said Florida was still deserted, even though there hadn't been a big hurricane in twenty years, most of the Americans still didn't trust it as a place to live. Be like moving to another planet for a Polynesian, the climates right, but I don't like it, and I don't think anybody else will either.

What to do? What to Do? Yazuli Nik'e mused as Ben's attention turned to Taea and past her to the approaching afternoon in Noa Ville and the anticipated evening he would share with her sipping absinth at their favorite sidewalk café on the village quay.

Finite'

b

Appendix
Quick Survival Guide for the End of
The Fossil Fuel World

1. Buy a home in the country: Small town, co-operative community un-obtrusive quiet neighborhood: If you can't afford to move now and you are not altruistic you can rent it out, then evict the tenant when the time comes. The alternative is to use it as a second home, which is better for security as you can stock it up with supplies. Look for an area with proven and hopefully diversified agricultural capability.

2. Localized sustainable energy: Local energy co-op based on hydro and or biomass gasifier, and or geothermal: If none of these exist in the area you choose, get active in the community and try to get them installed. The alternative is an area with proven natural gas, coal, oil, or wood reserves. If nothing else plant or buy trees.

3. Reliable clean freshwater. Shallow well or spring is best; have it tested for bacterial contamination. Never ever buy land in the country without proving it has good water first. Avoid wells that are more than 200' deep or rated at less than five gallons per minute. Look for running water in the area that can be advantaged for energy or other purposes. If you buy on a lake look for areas with reliable wind, for wind pumping.

4. Rural House and Site: Avoid flood plains, oceanfront, steep cliffs, or major fire hazard areas. Look for a basement or other secure area for storage of supplies and retreat, and some fertile land for growing food. Incorporate or retrofit with passive heating and cooling features. Look for local firewood or coal, but not next to the house. If you have a septic tank make sure it is big enough, and take care of it. Flush no feminine products, or harsh chemicals, and feed it, a half pound of hamburger or commercial septic health product once every few months. Install the simplest possible solar water heater.

    5. Transport: Buy a small motorcycle, or ATV for emergencies. This next part is difficult right now but will get easier as time goes on. Get a small pickup with a small high mileage engine. You want diesel or compressed liquefied gas, diesel because it can use the greatest variety of fuels, including bio-diesel, and because diesel will be a priority for trucking, tractors and basic infrastructure support. LNG because as time goes on biomass gasifiers with liquefaction plants will be installed across the country, and will most likely become the available fuel. These types of vehicles are also the easiest to retrofit with onboard 'gazogene' units, which you can run on wood chips. For survival avoid hybrids right now as the batteries will need replacement long before the rest of the vehicle wears out. Also do not discount the value of a strong mountain bike, a horse, or a good pair of boots.

    6. Fuel: If the small town or anchoring community does not currently have it get it installed. That is a tank farm for storage of diesel, propane and other fuels. Normal gas station tanks are far too small, and it's better to set aside a community area for this purpose, as residential storage is dangerous.

    7. Tools: Either make sure a full compliment of tools are available through community rental, or buy everything you will need, store them and keep them in good repair.

    8. Protein: Does the area have enough lands for beef, do the streams produce fish, will your chickens be able to survive the winters, and are there enough forests to support game? Agriculture and animal husbandry will not cease to exist, but protein will become very expensive in real terms. If it has to come from a long ways away it will be very expensive indeed.

    9. Security: Will you fit into the community? Is there or can there be a community? Is it far enough away from population hazards? Is the climate going to go on being reasonable?

    10. Economic Security: Is the local anchoring community serviced by railroad tracks? Are they in good shape? Is there any kind of economic foundation, beyond agriculture? If not can it be installed in a viable way? For instance if there are cattle somebody can make shoes, if there is cotton somebody can make clothing, if there is coal somebody can mine it, if there is a lot of energy locally somebody can make bicycles or even computer chips. In the new world, local energy abundance is directly equivalent to economic health. This includes large forests.

11. Health Care: In the new world people will have to be satisfied with less. You can get by with a local doctor that is actually willing to make a personal diagnosis, you don't really need million dollar MRI scanners, and huge hospitals, but you do need to ask your local government to stock non perishable supplies of vaccines, antibiotics, and other important medical supplies.

12. Common Sense and Homework: Use it and do it. Do not assume everything in this book will happen literally the day after tomorrow, do not throw your life away without careful consideration, but instead use this material as a guideline to assist in planning and anticipating the steps you may take to provide a reasonable future path for your life. It is a certainty that many of the things detailed in this book will happen, it is less of a certainty as to how soon or how bad they will actually be. Indeed if by some miracle a major portion of the human race paid attention to the material in this book and others like it, and took all the steps to address the issues, then there is a slight chance that almost none of the bad things will happen and that the world will end up gradually turning into a paradise model of Arcadia. However, it is a certainty it is better to be prepared than to be caught unaware.

Io Ora Na, e' Maruru…

Printed in the United States
38347LVS00005B/151